G4

OUR WAY

by G4

with Darren Henley

First published in Great Britain in 2005 by
Virgin Books Ltd
Thames Wharf Studios
Rainville Road
London
W6 9HA

A catalogue record for this book is available from the
British Library.

ISBN 1 8522 7279 1

The paper used in this book is a natural, recyclable product
made from wood grown in sustainable forests. The
manufacturing process conforms to the regulations of the
country of origin.

Designed by Button PLC

Printed and bound in Great Britain by The Bath Press, CPI Group

Picture credits: courtesy of Simon Fowler, Wil Rosser, Thames/Syco

Contents

I T was a Saturday night in December 2004. A group of four stylish twenty-something male singers had just given the performance of their lives in front of a prime-time television audience of millions. The applause in the studio was deafening.

Was this just another typical manufactured boy band doing their thing, hoping to make it big on a Saturday night talent show?

No, these four young singers were different. All of them had spent years training to a rigorously high standard as classical musicians and all had graduated from one of Britain's finest musical academies just a few months before.

Looking back, the lyrics of two of the songs that G4 sang on that fateful Saturday night seem so very apt. In Queen's 'Bohemian Rhapsody', the epic rock anthem that was to become G4's signature piece, the band sung: 'Is this the real life? Is this just fantasy?' And in their emotionally charged version of Radiohead's 'Creep', they asked: 'What the hell am I doing here? I don't belong here.'

Just three months later, the answer to those questions was proven beyond doubt when G4's debut album became the fastest selling release of the year, going double platinum in under a month. Few, if any, classically trained artists have crossed over into the pop-music world with such great success in such a short period.

G4's tale is one of four young music students' fantasy becoming a reality. Their huge achievements and consistent success since they first burst on to our television screens show that they did belong there on that stage that night. Their musical talent earned them the right to be there; and it continues to shine through to their millions of fans.

In their own words, this is the remarkable story of Jonathan Ansell, Michael Christie, Matthew Stiff and Ben Thapa. Together, they are G4.

Introduction

ALTHOUGH we spent many long hard years learning how to be musicians, even the most optimistic among us would never have dared hope that our success would come either as quickly, or in such a big way, as it has done. Being in the group has helped us to achieve all of our dreams in a way that we would never have thought possible.

We are often asked how and why we got together. The origins of G4 are rooted firmly in our time at music college. When we started out as a group, life was not about millions of people watching on television, sell-out concert dates or record-breaking CDs. It was all a bit simpler back then. But it was nowhere near as much fun.

To discover the genesis of G4, we need to wind the clock back to 2002. It all started because the Guildhall School of Music Drama which we all attended runs an external engagements system for students in the third and fourth years. It allows everyone to earn a bit of extra money singing for corporate events or as soloists for choral society concerts and helps give students a fighting chance of staying the right side of the bank manager. As well as auditioning as soloists, we also decided to get together as a group singing in the barbershop style. We ended up doing a lot of livery dinners because the Guildhall has strong connections with the City of London. It was here that we were given the chance to put everything we had learned into practice.

Basically we did it to earn some pocket money and because we loved to get out there and sing in front of audiences. When we saw how successful it could be, we decided to go out busking as well.

It was a great experience to have people stop and listen to us making music on the streets. It was very organic – much more so than standing up on a stage.

If we turned up to sing as soloists in an oratorio for a local choral society, people had gone to the concert to hear their local choir, rather than us. So they didn't necessarily have to like what we did. However, if someone stopped to listen to us on the street because we somehow managed to draw him or her into what we were singing, it was a more exciting relationship.

It gave us a different sort of buzz when we knew that all the people there were rooting for us. We make the same connection now when we stand on stage in front of concert hall or theatre packed full of our fans. Nothing beats singing live to our fans.

Looking back at both the busking and the gigs that we did then, we had the most amazing reception. Having said that, if we had gone along to a record company there was almost no chance that

G4 are born

they would have signed us up on the spot. We needed *The X-Factor* to get that exposure and, because we were so different, we had to convince the public that we were genuine. We needed people to believe in us, to feel comfortable with us and understand where we were coming from before they would be prepared to buy into us. If they were not quite sure about us as singers or as people, then they would have said 'No thanks' and walked away, just like one or two people used to do when we were out busking.

In December 2003, when Jon and Mike were out busking Christmas carols in the street, one or two celebrities stopped by and put some money in their hat, including Gwyneth Paltrow and James Nesbitt. We bumped into James at Dublin airport more than a year later and he remembered us as buskers, rather than as G4. When we saw him again a few months after that at the London Restaurant Awards, he mentioned our busking to us again.

Matt joined the barbershop quartet in January 2004, when our original bass left. The sound of his voice was just so cool and singing the songs became much more fun when you heard his big bass sound.

At around that time, we were asked what our name was as a group. Up until then, we'd just been known as 'the barbershop quartet from the Guildhall'. By that time, most of what we sang wasn't really traditional barbershop material because we had very soon broadened out the repertoire to include a cappella arrangements by Mike of 'Bohemian Rhapsody' and 'The Lion King'. The organisers of one particular gig insisted that we have a proper name. We didn't have a clue what to call ourselves, so we went through all sorts of options, including taking the first letter of everyone's name, but none of them quite worked. Then we came up with G-Force, which over time changed into G4 – short for the Guildhall Four. We had no idea at the time just how important having a short, snappy, memorable name would become to us in the future.

'There are only so many jobs around where you can express yourself as an individual and we're very fortunate to be in one of them.' – BEN

The X-Factor:
The Auditions

P EOPLE often talk about the power of television. But it's only when you have personally experienced life on a programme like *The X-Factor* that you can truly understand how pervasive it can be as a medium. The show gripped the nation and we were in the thick of it. But, unlike a soap opera, here the drama was completely genuine. There were no actors going home at the end of the day to enjoy evenings with their families.

As we were propelled further through the competition, our lives were played out in front of the nation. We were playing a high-stakes game of real-life jeopardy, which wasn't staged. It was happening right at that moment as the people at home were watching in their living rooms. Throughout the competition, there were winners and losers, but the longer everyone stayed in contention, the closer they came to fulfilling their dream.

'I'm not really an early morning person at all. I'm like the guy on the Kellogg's cornflakes advert – Neanderthal man before he's had his bowl of cornflakes. So every time we do breakfast TV, it's tough getting up. But then you think: 'But I'm on TV – how cool is that?' – BEN

It was around April 2004 that we first saw the television ad for *The X-Factor*. Simon Cowell was launching the biggest talent show in British television history. For the first time, they were accepting fully formed groups into a reality TV show. A friend of Matt's mum told him about the competition and Jon, who was an avid television viewer at the time, wrote down the number and called in. In all honesty, we thought it would be a bit of a waste of time. All they asked us to do was to leave our details and we decided that there was no chance at all of them ever getting back to us.

Then, a couple of months later, Jon was called on his mobile by one of the researchers from the show and we were asked to come for an audition at eight o'clock one morning. We were all buzzing with excitement and spent hours rehearsing what we would sing. We presumed that as we had been told to arrive at eight o'clock, we would be performing straight away. We knew that we couldn't risk being late, so we all went round to Matt's flat and stayed there the night before. We were up at a stupidly early time the next morning so that our voices had time to wake up for the audition.

Then we travelled over to Wembley, where the auditions were being held in the conference centre. To our surprise, we discovered that there were a few hundred other people who were also given eight o'clock as their arrival time.

We didn't know what to wear – after all, we weren't a pop group. We still thought of ourselves as being a barbershop ensemble at the time. In the end, we dressed in the same suits and black shirts that we would normally have worn to a classical gig. We knew instantly that we didn't really fit in at all in the queue of outlandish people. There was a transsexual up at the front as well as cute girls wearing virtually no clothes, whom we couldn't take our eyes off. There were all sorts of extroverts there, but alongside them were other people, who looked shy and terrified. It was a massive mix of personalities – a real mishmash of humankind.

A researcher called Freddy approached us and looked down at his clipboard. We would get to know him very well over the next few months, but at the time he was just another of the scores of producers, researchers and cameramen who were swarming around the building. Freddy asked us a series of questions about ourselves and we were almost instantly interviewed on camera. We think that as soon as they found out that we were classically trained, they knew that we were going to be an interesting story and that we would either crash and burn, or would go further in the competition.

The level of activity going on around us was amazing and we watched in awe as people were filmed jumping about and doing the splits.

We whispered to each other about not being quite as exciting as that. We were seriously wondering if we were going to get anywhere at all in the competition. As well as the more over-the-top individuals, there were some lovely people who spoke to us. Many of them had come on their own from miles away. We were all united together in the same place with the same crazy dream. The contestants were marked out from the production team by the large numbers stuck on our clothes to show the producers who we were. There was a strong bond of camaraderie because it was so early on in the competition that nobody was set directly against anyone else in the way that they were in the final stages.

We waited for our number to be called. By now, it was hours after eight o'clock, so that ridiculously early start had ended up being completely unnecessary. Eventually, we went through for our very first audition but before we walked through the doors, we were interviewed on camera. We were quickly learning that whatever we did always involved having an interview first. With that done, we were allowed in for our audition. There was one lady sitting in the room – a producer called Helen. As soon as we started singing, her face lit up. She tried to stop us after about thirty seconds, but as classical musicians, we had never sung just part of a song at an audition, so we carried on in the way we had been trained to do. We were used to our teachers or examiners waiting until right at the end of the performance before they gave us their comments. None of us had ever been stopped midway through, so it felt incredibly odd. We'd done a minute or so and she knew she wanted us to stay in the competition at that point, but we valiantly kept on going regardless. Eventually, we stopped and she

said, 'Well done. Here's your red letter, which gets you into the next round.'

We ran out of the room cheering and waving the red letter around our heads. Once again, the cameras followed our every move. Hardly any red letters had been given out at that stage, so some people looked at us a bit enviously. The letter told us that we had to come back on a certain date – scarily, it was the day before our final recitals at college. Obviously, there is a lot of preparation needed for those performances and so we pleaded with the producers to allow us to move our second audition to another date that week. As soon as we left the building, we phoned our families and friends to tell them the good news.

We kept things pretty much the same for our second audition – with the same suits, same shirts and even the same song. After all, it had worked the first time and we didn't want to decrease our chances. This was the final producer round, before the show proper. But before we had that second audition, the judges all came out to talk to all the competitors in the waiting area. It was amazing to see Simon Cowell, Sharon Osbourne and Louis

Walsh standing there in front of us. They told us that if we got through the next round, then we would get to meet them. They underlined their determination to be very strict and said that they weren't going to let any weak performances through. If we then passed that third audition, we would move on to the boot camp round. We had no idea what that meant at that point.

As they talked, Simon stood there puffing away on a cigarette throughout, which made us smile, because we were of course standing in a room with signs saying STRICTLY NO SMOKING on every wall.

The judges disappeared and, after another long wait, we were called for the second producer round. This time, a camera filmed us in the audition and there was a group of other producers watching us on a monitor in the corner of the room to see what we looked like televisually. Again, they stopped us midway through our song and told us we were into

the judges' round. There were more interviews and then a few more hours of waiting.

When we sang for the judges, everything was so different from the previous rounds, and a researcher showed us a diagram of how the studio would be set up. They told us where to stand, where the judges would be sitting and which door to walk in and out of. We were nervous wrecks by this time and so were grateful for all the help we could get. We found ourselves sitting on the bench outside next to Steve Brookstein. We later found out that he had been recalled by the judges because they wanted to hear him for a second time before deciding whether to put him through. It was an amazing coincidence that out of 50,000 people in *The X-Factor*, the final two acts sat next to each other at this early part of the competition.

At this stage, we met for the first time the lovely Kate Thornton, who presented the main ITV1 *X-Factor* programme. She interviewed each of the contenders on their way in and out of the judges' grilling. Steve was in with them before us, and when we heard that he was through to the next round, our spirits fell because we knew that they weren't going to let that many people through. We feared that the

law of averages would be against us. Kate wished us good luck as we walked through the doors. It was a nerve-wracking moment. We lined up in front of the judges, who looked on expectantly.

Simon broke the silence by telling us that we looked like a bunch of bankers, before asking Jon why we had come along. In the stress and excitement of the occasion, he replied: 'Well, it's not

'He pushed me until I was just on the edge and I managed to hold it, but then I left the set and I was in pieces. Mike patted me on the shoulder and said, 'Calm down, mate. It's all right.' But as soon as I saw Kate and she asked us how it went, I just burst into floods of tears. I got a big hug from Kate. In fact, my uncle reckoned I only kept on crying so that I would get a hug from her in the first place. People have ridiculed me for shedding some tears, but all of my close friends and family are not scared of showing their emotions and, at the right time, they will do it.' – JON

that far to come is it?' He thought Simon was asking why we'd come to Wembley, rather than why we'd come along for the audition.

'That's not a good way to start,' said Louis ominously.

Anyway, we started to sing and we could see the look on their faces change. Suddenly, they all seemed far friendlier towards us. We were so focused on the judges that we completely failed to notice a whole load of producers and researchers who were sitting out of shot of the camera on our left. This group included some people who would become very important to us later on: Claire Horton, the programme's series producer, Richard Holloway, the executive producer and Ashley Tabor, who would end up being our manager alongside Louis.

We sang 'Bohemian Rhapsody' and, when they asked us to stop, Simon told us it was very good. Each of the judges gave their comments, which were positive, and then Sharon asked if she could hear another song. Simon said that they didn't need to, but Louis agreed with Sharon and so we sung the start of 'The Lion King'. Simon picked out Jon and really complimented his voice. This was the first of many times that he ended up crying on national television.

They were tears of happiness though because we were through to the boot camp round. Before we left the building, we were interviewed for the first time by Ben Shepherd, who was presenting *The X-Factor Xtra*, which was running on ITV2 alongside the main programme. At that point, we were still allowed to tell our friends and relatives what was going on, so there was another frenzy of telephone calling as soon as we got outside.

A few days later, we packed our bags for a two-day stay at the Hilton Hotel in Angel in North London. None of us was quite sure what to expect. At that time we knew that Simon, Sharon and Louis would each be working closely with one of the three categories in the competition: the younger performers, the older performers and the groups. We still didn't know which judge would be paired up with which category though.

We turned up and checked in. At the time, it was a novel experience for us to be in a hotel room. The rooms had a TV and a minibar in the corner. We were told that if we raided the drinks cabinet we would have to pay for it, although we all thought that it would be quite cool to be able to say that we had drunk something out of the minibar. Even at this relatively early stage of the competition, we were experiencing things that we had never before come across in our lives.

We were told to go downstairs to gather together with the rest of the contestants. As we looked around the room, we saw all these good-looking, well-styled people. We, on the other hand, had just turned up in T-shirts and jeans – exactly what we would normally wear to college.

The producers talked to us and told us that nothing was happening that night and that we would each be given an allowance of ten pounds to go out to buy our dinner. They gave us strict instructions to be ready in the foyer, having finished our breakfast, by eight o'clock the following morning. It all seemed highly regimented, but we loved that because of our classical-music training. It took a bit of getting used to for some of the other contestants though. It turned out that during all of these early rounds, we were always the first people to turn up and were sometimes the only people to be on time. We have our teachers at the Guildhall to thank for that. They had constantly told us 'If you're late, you won't get work' and 'If you're not there on time, I'm not going to teach you.'

We went out that night and had dinner at a Thai restaurant. As we were sitting there eating, one of the researchers came to see us. They had taken Polaroid pictures of all of the contestants so that the cameramen could identify us more easily, but ours had failed to come out properly and they needed another one. It meant that right the way through the series, the crew's picture of us had a large Thai sculpture in the background, rather than the plain white wall that everyone else's had.

We got up early the next morning and enjoyed the vast – and, more importantly, free – cooked breakfast that was laid on in the hotel. This was pure luxury for us students. Then we walked to Angel Studios, which was just down the road from the hotel. Along

with the other contestants, we were directed to sit down and wait in a large empty room. By now, we were starting to get used to the waiting game and we learned very rapidly that nothing happens quickly in the TV business.

As we all sat there twiddling our thumbs for ages, with nothing much to do, everybody checked out everybody else in the room. Suddenly, someone started singing and then a few other people joined in. We all sat there in silence until Matt pushed us quite strongly to sing one of our songs. There were cameras roaming around and some people were clearly playing up to them. Eventually, we started to practise and gradually the noise level rose ever higher until everyone was rehearsing their own personal audition song.

All that we had been told at this point was that we would need to have one song prepared for the two days. We decided to sing 'Bohemian Rhapsody' once again. All of us were determined to sing it right to the end at some stage during the competition!

We were asked to perform something for Ben Shepherd to use on the ITV2 programme and so we sang 'The Lion King'. At that stage, nobody had heard anyone else in the room perform and so we felt a little exposed singing a cappella in front of them. But still, it was the way we normally performed, so we were probably more comfortable doing it than other people there might have been. As we sang, everyone else started to clap along and we felt quite chuffed with the response.

We carried on waiting and it was a couple of hours before anything meaningful happened. Then we were ushered into lines and told that in a minute or two, we would find out which of the judges was going to be looking after our category. A lot of people sneaked off for a quick toilet break in the hope that they would get a glimpse of the judge in a corridor. There was more waiting and the levels of anticipation were starting to rise. Suddenly, a battalion of cameras appeared all at once and took up positions right around the room – some of them were even up ladders. We were all told to be quiet and the big door at the end of the room burst open. We all strained to see which judge it was, but it turned out to be a producer running in with a spare battery for one of the cameras. The door closed and everybody was quiet again. This happened several times and it really

tested our nerves.

Then, suddenly, it opened and there was Louis Walsh and his on-camera team: Linda Martin, who would work with us on choreography; Faye Sawyer, who would be our stylist; and Dave Laudat, who would be our vocal coach. Everybody cheered and we were delighted to have Louis looking after us because of his huge success with groups such as Boyzone and Westlife.

A couple of hours later, we began to file upstairs for our first auditions in front of Louis. There was a huge staircase, where we all sat waiting. Regular interviews on camera punctuated the long periods of sitting around doing nothing. When we reached the top of the stairs, each of us was interviewed and then we were interviewed again before we walked into the room where Louis and the team were waiting.

We sang 'Bohemian Rhapsody' and then went back downstairs to the main room again. It seemed to have gone well. By this time, the levels of camaraderie between the contestants had risen again. Everyone seemed to suddenly realise just how much cool music there was in the room. It was

THE X-FACTOR: THE AUDITIONS | 25

certainly very diverse: pop, R 'n' B, soul and then there was us, whatever we are!

We kept on chatting to another group during the day. The fact that we were two groups of four guys meant that we had something in common. They were extremely good looking and well styled. In fact, they had the perfect boy-band look. They asked us to sing 'The Lion King' again and, this time, they added different sounds and harmonies into the gaps – one of them was brilliant at beat-bopping. Suddenly, other people in the room came over and started adding in their own stuff. At that point, it all kicked off and the whole room was either listening or had joined in our song. When we finished there was some amazing applause, so we launched into 'Bohemian Rhapsody' and, because it is one of those songs where everybody knows most of the words, they all sang along with us.

Next, Voices with Soul, who eventually went

through to the live finals, sang one of their songs and everyone joined in. Like us, they were a bit different from the other acts, so we were drawn to them. They are such a laugh – three incredibly charismatic ladies. The other eventual finalists, Pete and Emma, who make up Two To Go, then performed. Pete got his guitar out and, once more, everyone else in the room joined in with their songs. Pete plays the guitar like a piano, with it laid out across his lap and using his left hand to press down the frets and his right hand to pluck the strings. He sat in the middle of this big circle of competitors with everybody singing along. It had become a massive jamming session and ended up being one of our biggest memories of the whole *X-Factor* series: that room, where everyone was performing so many different styles of music simultaneously. In truth, we were all sharing our love of singing. For a while everybody forgot the competition and we were all just a room filled with

'The success has been so phenomenal in lots and lots of ways. Keeping relationships with friends and family the same has been hard sometimes, but it's really important that you keep honest with them and spend enough time with them so that they understand what's going on. Our success has been weird for us, but in lots of ways, it's weirder for them.' – JON

great singers, who loved our music.

After things calmed down a little, there were more interviews on camera. Then, we were told that the first evictions would take place. We were all lined up and, once again, there was a long silent wait. The tension was unbearable and it was too much for some people, who were sobbing away in the corner of the room.

We were each asked to come forwards and were then told whether we were through or not. We were relieved to have been one of the acts to make it a little further along the journey. For those of us at the next stage, we were then given a challenge where we had to write and perform our own song. The title was to be 'All the way' and we had to include the words 'chance', 'hopes', 'dreams' and 'anticipation' in our lyrics. Now, we might have had all the training at music college, but we had never worked together on a song in that way. And to make it just that little bit more pressurised, we only had an hour in which to do it. We noticed that with the other groups, someone would write down some lyrics and sing a

tune to it and someone else would sing a harmony to that and their song would just grow. We have now learned how to do that as a group, but at the time, we had not got a clue. After all, we had only been together for a few months. So, we felt under an incredible amount of pressure as we attempted to write the song. Each of us knew that if we messed it up, we might well be in the next set of people who would go home empty handed. It was awful to think that if that one song didn't work, then we could be leaving. It was a feeling that we would get used to again and again over the weeks that followed.

As the clock ticked away and the one-hour deadline edged ever closer, we slowly managed to get our song together. We have to admit that when we finally saw it played back on television, it was as camp as hell. Louis and the team told us that they liked it after the performance. We've spoken to Louis about it since and he told us that in actual fact he thought it was absolutely awful as a song, but that considering the constraints which had been placed upon us, it was good enough at the time.

It was the end of the first day of boot camp and there was another eviction at this point with some more people going home. We survived yet again and suddenly the group seemed much smaller. We knew that by the end of the following day, it would be much smaller still. The production team told us that we were not going to have an easy night of it though. We were instructed to pick one of three songs and to arrange it ready for performance at ten o'clock the following morning. Now, considering it was already late in the evening, all we were desperate to do at this point was to eat and sleep. But we all knew that we had to rise to the challenge. We picked the Boyz II Men song 'I Swear' from the three options given to us. The researchers handed out personal stereos and CDs so that we could hear the original versions. We still had not quite got used to the fact that there was no manuscript with musical notes printed on it, which is the classical rather than pop music way of doing things.

We were really lucky to have Ben with his perfect pitch. It meant that he was able to transcribe all of the keys and chords, which helped us to work the song up more quickly.

When they came in to film us preparing the song, the cameramen were interested to see how we were writing down actual notes and letters on paper, which was very different from the way the other groups were working.

We left the practice room that evening exhausted, but with a structure for the song, hoping it would be all right in the morning. We went out to get some dinner and then crashed out as soon as we could.

The next morning, we were up early to allow for some more time to arrange the song. As soon as we arrived at the studios, we started rehearsing again. But Jon kept forgetting the words. Ironically, he seemed to have particular trouble with a line that went: 'You can be sure I know my part.' Despite that, we passed the test and were still in with a chance of making it through to the next stage.

The last round came and we were asked to perform a song as a group, which included sections where each of us would sing on our own. Louis was keen to hear how strong a singer each person in the competition was, to make sure that a group wasn't hiding behind one or two talented people. We chose 'Danny Boy' and sung half a verse each. It was completely a cappella and it seemed unusual for the four of us to be singing together with no harmonies. It was also the first time we had sung wearing headphones in a sound studio. Louis and his team sat the other side of the glass listening to us through the speakers.

By now, virtually every time we moved, Kate Thornton would be there with a camera crew asking 'How do you feel?' and 'What do you reckon is going to happen?' We knew that only half-a-dozen groups would still be in the competition by the end of that day and we desperately wanted to be one of them.

We were told to wait on the staircase again and after yet more interviews, we were instructed to walk into the room where the panel were waiting for us. They sat on stools in a line along the far wall. We were told to line up against the opposite wall and then to walk forwards in a line on a cue from the director. We couldn't bear to look as they talked about us incredibly negatively, saying that we'd let them down here with this performance and that we hadn't known all the words there. They really put us down and we were convinced we wanted it so much

'I have silly techniques I use to remember words. I tap one finger on my leg to help me remember a line, or I push the ball of my foot into the floor to remind me of something else and I use images in my mind to help me remember different parts of a song. When we had to sing "I Swear", none of these techniques worked and I cocked up the words horrifically, but luckily the judges still seemed to love it.' – JON

at that moment, more than anything else in the world. If we didn't get through, it would have felt as if we had wasted all that energy, all that emotional turmoil and all that physical effort.

Then Louis said, 'You're in!' And all hell broke loose. We all hugged each other and then we all hugged Louis, Linda, Faye and Dave. We couldn't believe it. We were overjoyed. Amid all the celebrations, Dave Laudat said, 'Use this. Use this. It's your time.' We left the room and on the way out, even Ben shed a tear.

Before we went home, we were able to spend some time with Louis. He told us that he had liked us from the very start - news made us feel absolutely fantastic. He also described to us the journey that we would be going on over the next few weeks. He warned us not to tell our friends and family and said that the media would go to almost any lengths to discover who the finalists were. We had to keep the fact that we had gone through a secret because of the gap between when this section of the series was recorded and when it was to be broadcast. The producers wanted the final line-up on the programme to be a complete surprise to the viewers.

A few days later, we flew to Louis' house in Dublin for the next round. If we got through this stage, we would be taking part in the live finals every Saturday night on ITV1 for up to eight weeks – depending on how long we survived. We thought we would be a little different and, rather than wear suits, we dressed in jeans, a T-shirt and a jacket. Mike talked Jon into buying a very over-the-top velvet number, which he has never worn since.

We performed the Radiohead song 'Creep' for

Louis. He leaned over and said the immortal words, 'That could be a number one.' We were blown away and spent the rest of the day in a daze. Once everyone else had finished their performances, the panel told us that they knew who was going through, but that they were not going to tell us until the morning. There was no point in sitting around waiting and wondering in our hotel that night and drank more than a few pints of Guinness. It was good for all the acts to have the opportunity to let their hair down because, by that stage, we had all done everything we possibly could to affect our chances of getting through. We had a great night out and it was a tremendous release from all of the pressure of the previous few weeks.

The next morning, when Louis told us that we were through, we were overjoyed. The headaches we were nursing after the previous night's excesses simply evaporated away. We knew that things were now going to get really tough and that we had to mean business. We were introduced to Ashley Tabor, the man who would become our manager along with Louis. Ashley has become an incredibly important part of our lives since that moment, but at the time the only thing that struck us was that he had the most expensive-looking watch we had ever seen.

Our return from Dublin was co-ordinated by the production team as if it were a military operation that all of our lives depended upon. A producer took our mobile phones away from each of us so that we couldn't ring our friends and families to tell them the good news. A group of our nearest and dearest had been gathered together at Jon's house in Bognor and our announcement to them was to be a part of

the programme, so it needed to be captured by the camera crews. When we arrived in Bognor, we were surprised to find that we were not going straight to Jon's house. Instead, one of the producers took us down to the local pub, while the rest of the team filmed interviews with our friends and families.

We formulated a plan that when we got back to Jon's house, we would walk into the living room, count to ten really slowly, all look at Ben and then look up and shout, 'We're in!' We ended up waiting so long in the pub that perhaps we had one or two whisky and cokes too many. So, while three of us managed to return with sombre faces, Ben couldn't keep a big silly grin off his.

We walked into the room and everyone was gathered around us. The cameras were running. We started to count silently in our heads.

By the time we had reached 'four', Jon's mum couldn't bear the tension any more and pleaded: 'Just tell us!' But we carried on counting to ten and then shouted,
'We're in!'

Suddenly, the room seemed to get smaller as everyone jumped up. There was an amazing rush of emotion as the champagne corks popped. Telling the people closest to us that we were through was such a rewarding experience. Jon's sister had the funniest response, saying tearfully, 'He used to be the biggest prat in the world, but now he's the best brother ever.'

The emotions we felt right then were more extreme than anything we had ever encountered before. Matt quietly slipped away into the back garden and shed some tears, but the TV crews didn't notice, so they never managed to get any footage of him sobbing. That moment was effectively the end of what had been normality in our lives.

We all had to keep our success a huge secret to allow the broadcasts of the first few weeks of *The X-Factor* to catch up with reality. We desperately wanted to go around telling everyone how we had done, but we were under very strict instructions. It was almost unbearable, but we had to stay quiet for four long weeks.

Finally, we watched the show where we were told officially that we were through. Our mobile phones went ballistic as people called and texted to congratulate us. The relief of being able publicly to say the four words 'Yes, I am through' was amazing and gave us a huge sense of release. The very next day we moved into a hotel in the centre of London. The live finals were beginning the following Saturday night. We had no concept at all of how our lives were about to change.

G4 LIVE PERFORMANCE SCHEDULE

WEEK 1	**23/10/04**	**'Everybody Hurts'**
WEEK 2	**30/10/04**	**'Don't Look Back in Anger'**
WEEK 3	**04/11/04**	**'Hit Me Baby One More Time'**
WEEK 4	**13/11/04**	**'The Circle of Life'**
WEEK 5	**20/11/04**	**'My Way'**
WEEK 6	**24/11/04**	**'Somebody to Love'**
		'You'll Never Walk Alone'
WEEK 7	**04/12/04**	**'Bohemian Rhapsody'**
		'O Holy Night'
WEEK 8	**11/12/04**	**'Creep'**
		'Nessun Dorma'
		'Bohemian Rhapsody'

THE live finals of *The X-Factor* had it all: tears of joy and happiness swiftly followed by moments when we were plunged into the depths of despair. There were periods when our future seemed assured and other times when the outlook was bleak. It was a time when eyes and ears were assaulted from every side by a seemingly never-ending list of new experiences. It was, without doubt, the most terrifyingly exciting eight weeks of our lives.

This is the first time that we have shared our experiences both on and off stage. It was an amazing roller-coaster ride that we simply didn't want to get off. More than that though, it was the realisation of everything we had been working so hard to achieve over the previous years. We wouldn't have swapped this experience for anything else in the world. On 23 October 2004, we were a group of four music students. Eight long weeks later, on 11 December

The X-Factor:
The Live Shows

2004, we were four professional musicians. The dream had become a reality.

When the The X-Factor producers told us to pack for eight weeks, we knew that the only way we would be spending that length of time away from home would be if we stayed on the show right through to the final week. We just laughed it off because we honestly didn't believe that we would still be in contention at that late stage of the competition.

All three finalists in the group category – ourselves, Voices with Soul and Two to Go got on really well. There was no jealousy or bitchiness. Instead, we tended to look out for each other.

In that first week, everything and everyone around us was brand new and it was hard to take it all in. By the time the second and third week came around, we were getting into the swing of things. Thursdays, Fridays and Saturdays were the big three days in the week. We worked on our choreography on Thursdays, practising where we were to stand and who moved when and to where. Then on Friday, we were in the studios all day for a sound-check and to run through our songs on stage. We would also appear each Friday evening on the live ITV2 preview show, where viewers found out for the first time what we'd be performing the next day.

Saturday was, of course, the real killer because we would be up at seven in the morning and in the studios from eight o'clock. After breakfast, we would spend the morning running right through the show from top to bottom. Then we would break for lunch before the dress run in the afternoon. This was the full show, as it would be broadcast in the evening, except that the judges did not give their actual comments on the performances. Instead, they chatted away, filling the time allotted to them. Every single part of the programme was timed to absolute perfection because it was a live show.

We were live on ITV1 in the early evening for an hour and a bit, then we would be straight on to ITV2

for another hour, before the half-hour results show on ITV1 and then another final half-hour over on ITV2. There were always interviews to give and people to talk to after that. We were also able to snatch a few moments with our friends and families. We would finally get back to our hotel at about one o'clock the following morning, but even then our day was not quite finished. A producer was always waiting there for us to make sure that we each filmed a video diary looking back on the day, before we finally slumped into bed, emotionally and physically drained.

Each week, we needed to be back in the recording studio just nine hours later on the Sunday, so that we could plan our routine for the following week. Mondays, Tuesdays and Wednesdays were then taken up with vocal coaching, styling, photo-shoots and television, radio and newspaper interviews. It was like a never ending high-speed car chase – or, at least, everybody hoped that it would be never ending.

Because we were in a group, we needed to make sure that we allowed plenty of time to work on our vocal harmonies. The soloists were able to simply sing their chosen song with their own interpretation, but for us, we had to check out which combination of voices worked best at each point during the song. So each week, before the live show on Saturday, we had to put aside time to work on our songs for the following weeks, not knowing if we were actually going to be given the chance to sing them.

When we walked out onto the stage that first night ready to sing the REM song 'Everybody Hurts', it was like nothing we had ever experienced before. Although we had performed in front of crowds as big as the studio audience before, it had always been in a classical music context, where everybody would sit down quietly and enjoy our music. It was completely different to have people screaming for G4 and seeing huge G4 banners. We hadn't known what to expect up until that moment. We knew that each of the judges would back the finalists they were looking after – Sharon was coaching the younger soloists and Simon the older ones. Louis was still mentoring the three groups. Despite the firm allegiances of the judges, all three of them were very positive about us in that first week. It was not just the judges, but also the viewers watching at home that we had to impress though – and just like everyone else, we had only been given one minute and ten seconds in which to do it.

We had picked up a lot of new skills during that first week – the most important of which was how to use handheld microphones. It was the first time that we'd ever performed with them, having always worked completely acoustically before. When you sing without amplification, you can feel the vibe and you know the volume that you want to create. Suddenly, we were working with microphones and loudspeakers and a crowd that was screaming so loudly that we unable to hear ourselves sing. It was particularly hard for Matt, who has the lowest voice. Often, he was singing a bass line that competed directly against the bass guitar in the backing track. In the weeks that followed, we spent a lot of time working with the show's music producer, Nigel Wright, who helped us to create backing tracks that were slightly sparser, so that we could hear ourselves better.

The relief when Kate Thornton told us that we had stayed in that first week was enormous. Roberta was

the person who had to go, which surprised everyone because she was one of the favourites. By being able to vote, the public was in control of the outcome of each of the journeys that the various acts had set out upon. A vote for us meant that viewers felt that they had a say in what we did. So, when people come up to us now and ask 'How are you doing?' it's because we were on their television screens for three months and they have built up a rapport and a friendship with us. Somehow, they seem to relate to us in a way that is way beyond just a reaction to the music that we are performing.

In the second week, we sang the Oasis song 'Don't Look Back in Anger'. Simon said afterwards that it wasn't an obvious choice of song, although he did compliment our singing.

It was one of the tracks that we had a lot of discussions about as a group, but we ended up just going for it and, thankfully, we managed to get

through that week as well.

By the end of week three, everybody had an opinion on G4. If the first two performances had passed viewers by, then the idea of four guys standing up on stage in suits singing a cover version of the Britney Spears song 'Hit Me Baby One More Time' was certain to draw a response. It took real balls for us to get up there and do it. We wanted to make something completely different out of the song and it was a chance for Mike's and Matt's lower voices to become more prominent. It is still the song that kids ask us to perform more often than any other when we visit schools. And that night, when The X-Factor finished and Ant 'n' Dec started their show, they both stood there singing 'Oh Baby, Baby' in deep voices. Despite the controversy, the public really started to latch on to us at that moment. G4 had become a talking point. People were divided and we were the subject of heated discussions. Some loved the song; others hated it. But either way, it got them talking about us. We sang the song on our tour during the summer of 2005 and even then, when the audience heard that first bass line, the response was phenomenal.

By far our worst experience in the whole competition came in week four. It was a difficult show for us, because it followed on from 'Don't Look Back in Anger' and 'Hit Me Baby One More Time', where the judges had been divided about our song choices. We decided to come back with Elton John's 'The Circle of Life' from *The Lion King*, which was very much home territory for us. Suddenly, the judges were all back completely behind us, saying that we had chosen the right song and were singing it in the right way.

The public didn't seem so sure though. In the results show, there were just three acts left on stage: ourselves, Voices with Soul and Cassie. Two of these acts were going to have to sing to stay in the competition and one would be safe. The only certainty was that one was going home before the end of the programme. We didn't know which category we fell into and were angst ridden during the commercial break in the middle of the show. Louis came over to us and tried to reassure us that he was certain we would be safe.

When Kate announced that it was Cassie who was safe, we were devastated. It meant that the only way we could stay in the competition was by knocking out our best mates Voices with Soul. It ended up with Louis being put in the horrible situation where he had to choose between his two remaining acts, as we each had one vote apiece from Simon and Sharon. Poor Louis had been in exactly the same position the week before, when he'd had to choose between Voices with Soul and Two To Go. He eventually picked us and we were safe for another seven days.

'The most bizarre experience that I have had since I joined the band was in the third week of the live finals in Covent Garden in London. I'd just come out of a bakery where I'd bought some food for dinner. In front of me was this girl wearing an Offspring hoodie, who must have been about sixteen and she had more metal on her face than an entire stainless-steel factory in Sheffield.

"You're in that opera band, aren't you?" she said.

"Yeah," I replied.

"I just want you to know that I love you guys and I'm voting for you every week. Before, I didn't really like opera. I thought it was a bit boring, but now I'm getting into it because of you guys."

Then she turned around and walked off. That people can have such diverse tastes in music is fantastic.' – BEN

We missed the girls from Voices with Soul. They were absolutely incredible and having to fight against them and knowing that one of us would go home as a result had been terrible. They are among the most generous, giving and friendly people that we've ever met. One of the great things about the past year is that we have come across so many different types of people, who we would never have encountered if we had not been a part of *The X-Factor*.

After we had been in the bottom two in the fourth week, we had a whole new lease of life on the show, with songs that really suited us. Up until then, we had been experimenting, but now was the time to really go for gold. We needed to find our best style and stick with it. Despite that, in week five, we were

convinced we were going to go home and so it seemed appropriate that the song we picked was the legendary Frank Sinatra classic 'My Way'. We had a choice on the Monday of that week: we could either take a day off and risk getting knocked out on the Saturday, or we could give it everything we had and do everything in our power to stay in the competition. So, we went to Lakeside shopping centre in Essex and gave a live performance, which was incredible. Matt and Mike visited schools in London, while Ben went back to Cambridge and Jon went to Bognor. We did so much promotion because we thought that if we were going to go down, we would do it fighting. It was one of the hardest working weeks of our lives and we knew that if we failed to get through, it would

all have been for nothing.

Nobody had ever done an a cappella song live on a mainstream Saturday-night entertainment show like *The X-Factor* before. We decided to go completely minimalist with our version of 'My Way' because viewers are so used to hearing the impact of a backing track with a strong beat. So, it was just four guys on stage, sitting on stools, singing without the track for the first half of the song. We went on that night thinking: This could be it. This really could be our last performance. Perhaps we felt more comfortable because we had nothing to lose. To our surprise, the audience in the studio seemed to respond well and even the crew told us it was the most successful song we had done so far. Despite all

of the encouragement, we were still convinced that we would be going home this time because we had been in the bottom two the week before.

When Kate called our name out ahead of all of the other contestants, it meant that we were safe. All four of us were engulfed in an amazing wave of relief. We went mad and jumped up and down, with Jon screaming so loudly that he completely lost his voice. At first we thought it would come back, but a couple of hours after the show, he was still unable to talk and the condition of his voice started to really worry us. He had managed to damage his vocal chords by shouting so loudly. We banned him from speaking for three days to see if the problem would clear up. He kept rigidly to the ban to the point

where he was not allowed to speak when we did an interview for Capital FM that week. Although it sounds humorous now, it was anything but funny at the time. We seriously considered whether we would have to pull out of the competition. Because we were G4, the idea of just three of us going on stage to perform seemed wrong. Luckily, Jon's voice slowly improved over the next few days and it was virtually back to normal by the middle of the week.

We knew that if we progressed through into week six, we would be able to sing two tracks. Out of all the acts on the show, we felt that the opportunity to perform twice in one programme would benefit us the most because of the diversity of repertoire that we could sing. We ended up picking the Queen song 'Somebody to Love' and the great Rodgers and Hammerstein classic 'You'll Never Walk Alone'. After we walked off stage from singing our second song, we all had tears in our eyes because we knew how close we had come to not being able to perform that week. It was the first time we had all become really emotional during a song. It would not be the last.

The response from the judges was positive, except for Simon, who, rather than giving a positive or negative view, decided to say that he did not really know what to make of it.

Jon decided to respond on the spur of the moment and told Simon how disappointing it was that he wouldn't give an opinion. Apparently this caused the votes to surge.

The viewers always enjoy seeing one of the acts answering back to Simon. We were back on stage for the results show and Kate told us that we were through to the semi-final.

It was Rowetta's turn to go home that week, which was difficult because she became very emotional. Her departure meant that the last girl was out of the competition and it was now all guys: ourselves, Steve Brookstein and Tabby. London taxi drivers always had a view on the competition whenever they drove us anywhere and, that week, all of the cabbies we met told us that it would be Tabby and G4 in the final. It turned out that they were fifty per cent right.

For our two semi-final performances, we chose 'Bohemian Rhapsody' and, as Christmas was fast approaching, the carol 'O Holy Night'. We had an incredible response from the studio audience as well as

'Louis is a really nice guy and, behind the scenes, he's so supportive to us. He really believes in us as a group and has not tried to change us as people. He's very driven about success and he believes we can be successful.' – MIKE

from Sharon and Louis. Simon was, however, once again non-committal about our performance.

Kate did ask him whether he thought G4 had done enough to make the final and he said that he thought we might have done. It was amazing for us to hear those words coming from him and we knew after we had walked off the stage that we had done as well as we could. If we were to go home that week, then at least we had given it our best shot.

The wait for the results show seemed to be particularly agonising that week. The minutes seemed to tick away at half speed. Finally, the results show began, but, even then, every last drop of drama was wrung out of the announcement. We hung desperately on every word that came out of Kate's mouth. When she finally told us that we had got through to the final, we went nuts again – but then it's true to say that we went nuts every week that we got through. It was great for Louis too because he had thought that his

competition was going to be over a few weeks before. All of a sudden, it was Sharon and Tabby who had gone from the competition, which was a big shock.

Saving 'Bohemian Rhapsody' until the semi-final was a masterstroke, although there was a real risk that we would never have sung it on television had we gone out in an earlier round. When we stood there on stage on one side of Kate Thornton with our rival Steve Brookstein on the other and she said, 'These are your X-Factor finalists,' the feeling was sensational and we all had goose-pimples. It was then that the realisation of what we were about to do gradually sunk in.

We had a hugely busy week, changing our minds about eight million times about which songs we were going to sing. We very nearly did 'Somebody to Love' but swapped to 'Bohemian Rhapsody' at the last minute. We had decided fairly early on that if we got that far, we would perform the Radiohead song

'What's great with us is that people have an opinion.
I'd much rather someone turned around and said,
"I hate G4 … I just don't get them," rather than not knowing how they feel about us. I think we're the musical equivalent of Marmite: people either love us or hate us. There's nothing in between.' – MIKE

'Creep' once again. But the question of what we should do for our third track had been preying on our minds. Louis and Ashley asked: 'Is there anything classical that you can do?' We started singing 'Nessun Dorma' and they shouted, 'That's it!'

We wondered how a piece of grand opera would be received on prime-time Saturday night ITV1 and it was a huge gamble. We decided to make it our first of the three performances and the audience went wild. They could so easily have said, 'What the hell is this?' But, fortunately, they liked it. It came with us on to our first album and has become a really major track for us. But the decision to sing it was actually made with Louis and Ashley in a tiny little dressing room in about five minutes just after we'd got through to the final week.

As we performed 'Creep' and 'Bohemian Rhapsody', we knew that the stakes were high, but by that stage we also knew that we had come a long way. That night was just the most intense series of high pressure moments and by the time the results show came and we were standing up on the stage at the end, we were just desperate to find out how we had done – as much as anything, to put ourselves out of the misery of waiting.

We're often asked if we felt like failures for being runners-up. In some ways we did, but in others ways we quickly realised that we were winners too. We had been told by loads of people that acts who come second in these reality television shows often go on to have bigger careers than the winners, but the ambitious side of us just wanted to win the competition. So, to come second was obviously disappointing to start with. But that night, Louis and Ashley introduced us to Rob Stringer and Ged Doherty, who run the record company Sony BMG and our lives changed completely. Louis and Ashley said, 'You're going to be signed, boys!' And they were right. So we weren't disappointed for long, thankfully.

In hindsight, it has been a launch pad for our journey as a band. We're thankful that it helped us, but we signed our record deal in our own right – we weren't guaranteed anything by finishing in second place. Not only that, but in Sony BMG we have one of the biggest record companies in the world working on our behalf. It's one of the many new parts of our life over the past year that we sometimes cannot quite believe.

That night, we appeared on the ITV2 show, which looked back on the whole series and then we had a few drinks with our friends and family who were there with us. It was great to finally spend time with them. Afterwards, we ended up in a bar near Piccadilly Circus with the ITV2 presenter, Ben Shepherd. A girl came rushing up to him in the bar and quite genuinely told him that he was the best singer in the band!

IT is impossible to underestimate the effect that *The X-Factor* has had on our lives. But it is only a part of the G4 story. Our success on the programme allowed us to continue to build our careers and to achieve more of our dreams. Ever since each of us can remember, we've had the desire to make a record that would touch millions of people's lives. Just three months after *The X-Factor* ended, that record was released. The response from the public was overwhelming and it catapulted us into the music industry big time. It seems strange really, because critics attempt to put our music into a single box all of the time, but no one quite manages to do it. We have been described as a classical boy band, an opera boy band, opera superstars, a barbershop quartet, a four-piece male ensemble. But none of these monikers seems to quite fit what we do. There is one thing that is for certain though: we have made a connection with the listening public. And that is what we always set out to do.

There are a huge number of benefits from being part of a group, rather than a solo act. In the music business, you often learn by making mistakes and it is impossible to underestimate the upside of having three other people around you whose honest feedback you trust.

We are constantly bouncing ideas off each other and it is extremely helpful having the support of other people experiencing the same thing as you, at the same time as you.

And that is particularly important when you're doing everything for the very first time.

We recorded our first album between the end of *The X-Factor* television series and the beginning of

The First Album

The X-Factor Tour. People were asking 'What's happened to G4?' because we were on everyone's TV screens every Saturday night and then, suddenly, for a few weeks, we disappeared. We used that time to record the vocals for our first album. We had set ourselves the target of bringing the finished record out in time for Mothers' Day, so we had to get everything done incredibly speedily.

We recorded all day together for about three weeks at Metrophonic, a lovely studio near Guildford, which is based in a converted stable block at the end of a garden. We worked with three great guys –

Graham Stack, Brian Rawling and Cliff Masterson – who taught us so much about singing in recording studios. There was a big house attached where we could chill out during the breaks.

The process of making an album was quite different from what we had expected. One person would record their vocals in the booth, while the other three sat in the control room outside, from where they would all chip in advice on the performance that was being recorded. In a way, each of us is a little budding record producer and, on occasions, the levels of critical analysis coming from the control room could be quite intense. It is technically quite complicated because we sang one at a time and layered our voices on most of the tracks, so diction and coming on and off consonants at the beginning and end of each word is crucial. We were also lucky enough to work with the legendary producer Trevor Horn on 'The Circle of Life' and 'My Way'. We recorded those tracks in a very large studio in London surrounded by sixteen microphones, which was another new experience for us.

While we were working on the album at Metrophonic, we stayed in Guildford and went out for dinner together every night. Spending so much time with three other people can be testing at times, but it is unquestionably part of being G4. It is strange because we probably see more of each other than most husbands and wives do. If you said to anyone that they had to spend twenty-four hours a day, seven days a week with their spouse, they would probably run a mile. And that is with someone with whom they are infatuated. So, we get on incredibly well considering.

The first day that our album was out in the shops, we were recording a programme for Classic FM and we went into the big HMV on Oxford Street in London and each bought a copy on the way to the studios. We put our CDs on the counter and the assistant instantly registered who we were and gave us the most disapproving stare. We have all signed the outside of the albums we bought that day and have pledged to never break open the seal. We are hugely keen on keeping our heritage, so that we have mementoes of everything once our lives slow

'The day the album came out, my dad went to Tesco and bought it. He rang me up from the car park outside the supermarket and left a message on my answerphone. He was clearly sobbing: "It's your dad here. I've got your disc and I'm so proud." All the waiting, the whole show, everything building up, and then, finally, it was there – our dream – to have our record out in the shops. It's very easy to take things for granted, but the realisation of what the end product means to you and that spontaneous reaction from people who are so dear to you is really moving.' – JON

down. We have even kept the pens with which we signed our album deal.

Our record company, Sony BMG, is quite some machine and we are very lucky to be looked after by Nick Raphael and Jo Charrington, who have let us become far more involved in the making of our album than we had ever dreamed possible.

We are constantly meeting new people from Sony BMG who are working on helping our records to be a success in one way or another. The number of individuals involved in making an album is phenomenal. It has given us a real insight into the music industry. We had no idea how many different jobs there were. It is one of those industries where you have to get on the inside before you can really understand how it works. Going to see the careers advisor at school, they would have had no idea at all, but our advice to anybody considering a job in the record business is to stick at it because only the most tenacious people are allowed in through the door.

In the first week after our album was released, we sold 245,000 copies and we turned around to Louis and Ashley, our managers, and Nick and Jo from Sony BMG and asked, 'Is that good?'

'Are you guys serious?' came back the reply.

'We've go no point of reference,' we said.

Our naivety must have seemed charming in some ways, but it pretty much sums us up. We had never even considered analysing the number of albums that other artists sold, hoping that some day G4 could suddenly get an album deal and it would all work out. It has just happened to us and is just one of those incredible experiences that we never saw coming, but we have had the most incredibly creatively rewarding time doing it. We were even more amazed as the total number of album sales continued to rise and, at the time of writing this book, our debut album has now gone double platinum, which means that more than 600,000 copies have been sold.

In that first week, we went straight into the charts at number one and it was like being back on the television on a Saturday night again.

We were in Scotland when Ashley called to tell us that he wanted us on a conference call. On the other end of the line was Louis, Nick, Jo Brock and himself. We were with our brilliant tour manager, Gareth Russell, huddled around a mobile with the speakerphone on. When we heard the words 'You

As used by Top Of The Pops and Radio One

Produced in co-operation with the BPI and Bard, based on a sample of more than 4,000 record outlets
© The Official UK Charts Company 2005

MUSICWEEK
The Official UK Charts 12.03.05

ALBUMS

			Sony Music
1	N	**G4** G4	Syco Music
2	6	**IL DIVO** IL DIVO	Universal TV
3	10	**TONY CHRISTIE** DEFINITIVE COLLECTION	A&M
4	17	**THE CARPENTERS** GOLD – GREATEST HITS	Polydor
5	2	**SCISSOR SISTERS** SCISSOR SISTERS	Island
6	3	**KEANE** HOPES AND FEARS	EMI
7	25	**MATT MONRO** THE ULTIMATE	Epic
8	N	**JENNIFER LOPEZ** REBIRTH	Reprise
9	13	**MICHAEL BUBLE** IT'S TIME	Virgin
10	26	**PHIL COLLINS** LOVE SONGS	

are number one', we all jumped up in the air, screamed and hugged each other. We were just so thrilled because there had been so much hype about the album and we were really concerned about it failing to live up to its billing. It was bizarre to look down the list of acts in the record-industry magazine *Music Week* and to see all these famous people below us. Later, we found out that in that particular week in the USA, their number-one record was an album by 50 Cent, which had sold 188,000 copies. That meant that we'd actually sold more than the American number one, which we had trouble trying to comprehend.

We have been really lucky with everyone we have worked with. There has been nobody who we have met and then decided that we never wanted to work with again. We have come to rely very heavily on Jo Brock, who works in our management team along with Louis, Ashley and David Forecast. We used to have big diaries and Palm Pilots, but now we just have Jo on the other end of the phone. She always knows where we are and, more importantly, where we are supposed to be 24 hours a day.

At first, everyone working in our team probably saw us as a bit of a challenge because our album was like nothing they had worked on before. All of the engineers told us that they had never recorded an album so quickly. Since the summer of 2004, when everything really started to kick off for G4, we have been almost constantly performing or creating

music. In the end, we prepared as many as 25 tracks for our first album, some of which made it on and some of which we saved for the second album and other discs in the future. It is always very exciting to hear the final mix of each track and the day that we sat down to listen to our debut album in full for the first time was very special. We would imagine that it's somewhere close to giving birth to a new child. It gave us immense pride to sit there and think: That's us.

We have particularly enjoyed appearing on *Top of the Pops* and *CD:UK*. It is remarkable that we can be on programmes like that one day and then presenting a programme for Classic FM the next. That mixture has never been done before and it remains very important to us to be credible in both the classical-music and pop-music worlds.

If you had walked up to us two years ago and told us that we were going to be on *Top of the Pops*, we simply would not have believed you. It was awesome to be standing on that famous stage and to look around and see the signs around us, thinking: We're really here. Many of our friends called us to say 'We saw you on *Top of the Pops*' and our response was 'Yes, it's incredible isn't it?' But it didn't stop there. When our video for 'Bohemian Rhapsody' came out, it was played on the Box TV channel and in its first week of release, it went straight to the top of the most requested chart.

People see the glamorous side of what we do and

'Celebrity and stardom can be quite a costly hat to wear. It's not easy and you have to work hard, but if it goes well, the financial benefits can be great. There is the side of it where you become public property. For me, I'm happier having a quiet drink at a friend's flat, rather than going out to a party packed full of celebrities.' – MATT

they don't necessarily understand that we spend a lot of our time leading very normal lives. Regardless of what happens in our careers, we have still got the same friends as before. We turn up more often than not in the same places to have a drink as we used to and we still all enjoy the same hobbies.

It can be weird getting recognised when you are shopping in the supermarket or going to watch a movie at the cinema, but it is something that we have become used to.

After the initial shock, we realised that it was cool that our fans knew who we were because they are the very same people who are actually making our career happen.

They are the people who turn up to our gigs, buy our CDs and wait patiently for hours for us outside TV studios. And they will always be incredibly important to us.

We have had so many letters from schools saying that more boys have joined the choirs and that music teachers have set up barbershop quartets because of us. We're delighted that we have inspired people in that way. Some of the other letters we've had have also been incredibly moving. We had one note from a pensioner just after The X-Factor finished, saying how upset she was that we had been runners-up. She went on to say that she was prepared to give us her pension for a year so that we could make a record if we failed to be signed up by one of the big companies. The fact that people become so genuinely involved with what we are doing just amazes us.

We have made a lot of friends in the media as well. Lorraine Kelly has always been really supportive towards us when we have been on her show on GMTV. We saw her sitting on the next table to us when we did a presentation at the Sun's Wonder Mum Awards and she came over to chat to us. She's a really lovely lady, although we still find it weird that people like Lorraine, whom we were watching on TV when we were students, now know our names and know lots about us. It is slightly odd to turn up early in the morning to do a show that you know your mum is going to be watching at home anyway, regardless of whether you are a guest on the sofa or not.

Ant and Dec have also been very supportive of us and we had great fun working with them on their top-rating Saturday Night Takeaway show. As part of the Ant versus Dec feature on the programme, we

'Our fans remember the weirdest things about us. My mum was asked on camera very early on in *The X-Factor*: "What's the worst thing Jon does?"
And she replied: "His flatulence!" Even now, I still get cards talking about my alleged problem. It's amazing what people remember and how receptive they are to the smallest of details. ' – JON

had to teach them both to sing. It was a real laugh and they are both incredibly nice guys. We all performed with our arms in slings in sympathy for Dec, who had broken a bone doing a motorbike stunt on the programme a couple of weeks earlier.

It always shocks us when we meet celebrities who love what we do. We appeared on a legendary Irish television programme called *The Late, Late Show*, where the stunningly beautiful Caprice was also a guest. She was really friendly and invited us all out for a drink in Dublin, but duty called and we had to fly straight back to London, which was a real shame.

We were asked to take part in two Saturday night music shows, which were broadcast in the spring of 2005 on ITV1. *Queen Mania* and *Madonna Mania* featured a series of different acts singing the music of Queen and Madonna. We sang 'Bohemian Rhapsody' on the first programme and the producers asked us to sing 'Barcelona' as well. Some time before, Louis had suggested 'Barcelona' as one of the songs he wanted us to record and Nick and Jo from Sony BMG had already paired us up with the soprano Lesley Garrett to record it. We all knew and admired Lesley's singing from our days back at college. It was fantastic working with her and she was great fun. Our collaboration came out so well that we decided to put the track on to our second album and to feature it on our tour.

'Performing on a tour is quite physically grinding and you're on such a high after a concert that you just don't know what to do with yourself. It's fantastic to have such an enormous amount of support from our fans, but it can sometimes seem strange to come to terms with. You think: Hang on a second … has that really happened? And then you think: Actually, yes it really has. That's quite cool.' – MIKE

The Tour

JUST after *The X-Factor* finished on television, Jasper Carrott invited us to go up to the NEC in Birmingham to take part in his 2004 Christmas Cracker concert, which he puts on for charity. We performed 'The Lion King', 'Bohemian Rhapsody' and 'My Way'. We were told by Jasper that everybody in the audience had a tiny torch in their goodie bags and to encourage the audience to use them during one of our songs. It seemed

particularly apt on 'My Way'. We had never performed in an arena gig before and we were standing on stage singing completely a cappella, so we were not entirely sure what to expect.

Suddenly, there was a whole sea of people in front of us moving their torches, but they were out of time. So, we raised our arms in the air and the audience started to do the same thing in time with us. It sent a real tingle down our spines and we walked off stage

with big smiles on our faces. The experience of connecting with that many people while singing live is phenomenal. We had just been runners-up in *The X-Factor* and, that moment, standing there on stage in Birmingham, was the realisation that our dream to continue to perform live was coming true.

When you sense admiration like that from an audience who are responding to you in real time, it feels very touching to be standing there on stage.

We felt greatly inspired when we realised that we could captivate an audience in that way.

It was all the more special considering that we did it without dancers, without choreography and even without a backing track.

We have a classic saying: 'Tits and Teeth', which for some reason we use every time we are about to go on stage. It stems from photo sessions where we have to grin inanely at the camera for hours on end. We always say it as a group while waiting in the wings to go on stage. It has become our special little code, which means: 'Right … we mean business … time to perform.'

Photo shoots have become a big part of our new lives and that means that we get to work with many different stylists. How you dress can be hugely personal and some people react well to being styled and some don't. With ourselves, it is definitely a case of 'four heads are better than one'. It is even better still when we are able to work with people who have been trained in these things. They have an uncanny knack of seeing the potential of how each of us can look, no matter what state we are in at the beginning of the shoot. For example, Ben would never have thought of having red dye in his hair, but he did it all the way through *The X-Factor* and everyone commented on how great it looked. It is incredible when we turn up to a photo shoot and have someone do our hair and clothes. We see the pictures afterwards and invariably say to each other: 'Yes, it does look better than anything I could have managed for myself.'

To be on the road day in, day out, on *The X-Factor* Tour at the beginning of 2005 was absolutely incredible. All the venues were big stadiums, so the

crowds were massive. A lot of people from the audience came up to us after the shows and said, 'I wasn't sure I liked you on the show, but now that I've heard you singing live, I've changed my mind.' The joy of live performance was something that we were able to share on that tour and a lot of people were converted by what we did there.

We pride ourselves on live vocals and in giving an honest performance. That means that if we sing badly, the audience hears it and we have to take the rap for it. Maybe it is part of our classical training,

because when you are on an opera stage, you always sing live. At the Royal Opera House, singers are not given the chance to mime along to vocals on a pre-recorded track, so we have had the need to sing live drummed into us from an early age. It is strange for us to come into this industry and to see how many people do not sing live. In some cases, we can understand the reasons why they choose not to, but for us, as we are not a heavily choreographed band, there isn't any dancing around to get in the way of the vocals.

OMEBODY TO LOVE
LIFE ON MARS
CREEP
MY WAY
Costume change
ONE SWEET DAY
WALKING IN MEMPHIS
HERO
NEW YORK NEW YORK
BROKEN VOW
Costume change
BEACH BOYS MEDLEY
Costume change
YOU'RE THE VOICE
THE FIRST OF MAY (WITH ROBIN GIBB)
BARCELONA (WITH LESLIE GARRETT)
JERUSALEM
NESSUM DORMA
Costume change
MEDLEY - HIT ME BABY, ETC.
YOU'LL NEVER WALK ALONE
TO WHERE YOU ARE
Costume change

CIRCLE OF LIFE
BOHEMIAN RHAPSODY

The X-Factor Tour was a frantically busy time for us, because our first album was due to come out just a few days after the final concert. So, although we spent most of the time travelling about with the other eight acts on a huge tour bus, there were times when we had to zoom off to do promotional work for the album. On one frenetic day, we played a great concert in Glasgow, jumped on the sleeper train down to London, performed on *CD:UK*, did a radio interview and then drove straight back up to Sheffield to carry on with *The X-Factor* Tour that night. It was

absolute mayhem, but we were not bothered in the slightest. It was more of a challenge to see if the itinerary that had been planned for us actually worked.

In the summer of 2005, we were back on the road again with our own theatre tour. It was the first time that we'd had to hold an audience with a ninety-minute live set all of our own. Our old friends Voices with Soul were our support act and it was great to see the girls again.

There were some fantastic nights on that tour, but one of the most amazing highlights was singing to a

'People are very lovely and so excited to see and speak to us and that's very humbling because without them, we wouldn't be anything. We always try to stop to have a chat. I remember I met Sophie Ellis Bexter at college. She was really nice and signed a photo for me. I've always remembered that and told people about it.' – JON

sell-out audience at the Royal Albert Hall in London. We got a real buzz from being there. It's a venue that everyone knows and it's such a beautiful place to perform. It was incredible for us to be headlining there, rather than just a support act. Some absolutely huge stars have played there over the years and we never want to get to the stage where we're complacent about performing in venues like that. We were particularly proud that Robin Gibb and Lesley Garrett both sang live on stage with us. Neither had been billed in advance, so it was a special present to our fans, many of whom had travelled from all over the country to be there that night. Amazing!

NAME:	Michael Christie.
VOICE:	Baritone.
BIRTHDAY:	21 April 1981.
STAR SIGN:	Taurus.
BORN:	Redhill, Surrey.
MUSICAL INSTRUMENTS:	Piano and flute.
MUSICAL INFLUENCES:	Puccini, Richard Strauss, Manic Street Preachers, Amy Winehouse, Bryn Terfel and Thomas Hampson.
ALL-TIME GREATEST MUSICIAN:	Stevie Wonder.
WOULD MOST LIKE TO PERFORM WITH:	Renèe Fleming.
IDEAL WOMAN:	Natalie Imbruglia.
FAVOURITE FOOD:	Peanut butter and seafood – but not together.
FAVOURITE BOOK:	*To Kill a Mockingbird* by Harper Lee.
FAVOURITE FILM:	*Pete's Dragon*.
FAVOURITE WAY TO RELAX:	Composing music.
FOOTBALL CLUB:	Millwall when I was younger.
DREAM HOLIDAY DESTINATION:	Australia.
MOST ANNOYING HABIT:	Being late.
MOST OVERUSED WORD:	'Tired'.
JOB IF NOT IN MUSIC:	Sculptor.
WORST G4 MOMENT:	Being in the bottom two in the fourth week of *The X-Factor* up against our friends Voices with Soul.
BEST G4 MOMENT:	When our album went to No.1 and platinum in its first week. 'Time-keeping is always really important because there are four of us, but Mike is dreadful at it. We've tried to employ all sorts of strategies for getting him out of his flat on time. All of them have failed.'

Mike's Story

MY parents moved into our house in a small village on the border of Surrey and West Sussex just before I was born and it is the only family home we have had ever since. I lived there for eighteen years along with my mum, dad and two older sisters: Jane, who now lives in London, and Amy, who lives in Devon.

My dad now works as a bursar in a local school after many years working in IT. My mum is a computer programmer, but I remember when we were younger and she was in her twenties, she used to teach home economics. It was back when microwaves first came out and people discovered that you could even cook a sponge in them in a matter of minutes. She has done a variety of jobs that have taken her from home economics to computer programming.

I started off my education in a state school and later went on to public school and sometimes people give me stick about it. Basically, my parents had to work flat out to fund me through Reigate St Mary's and Ardingly College. I was awarded three scholarships, which helped to pay the fees. So when people look down at me for having been educated privately, I just think of the huge sacrifices that my parents made to send me there. I have never felt any pressure from Mum and Dad and they have always been supportive, telling me that whatever career I chose, they would be right behind me.

When I was growing up, I went through a long phase of wanting to be a vet. I did work experience with a local veterinary practice and loved it. I always grew up around animals. Although our house was suburban and a main road ran past the front door, it had fields for miles behind, so we had the best of both worlds. As a family, we often went to animal fairs and, when I was about eleven, I decided that I really wanted some chickens. I kept on hassling Mum and Dad and they told me that I would never look after them properly, so it would be unfair on the chickens for us to have them in our garden.

That didn't stop me though and I kept on

yes, I was cheeky, and yes, I was mischievous

my next door neighbour for 18 years

pestering them, faithfully promising to take good care of them. Eventually, I convinced my parents and we fixed up an old chicken house that had been sitting at the bottom of our garden for years. Dad and I attached a fox-proof run and generally made it habitable for our new arrivals. I started off with six standard chickens and then a few months later I came home from school and Mum had bought two little ducklings. We then started to breed them and, at one point, we had 25 chickens and ducks in the back garden, all with different names. We also bred rabbits, guinea pigs and fish and we always had cats and dogs. I think that this is where the idea of me being a vet came from. Although, once I realised how well you had to do at science subjects at school to get into veterinary college, I started to change my mind.

I really enjoyed music and did it as one of my GCSEs. When it came to choosing my A levels, I knew that I really needed to do subjects such as maths and physics to be able to be a vet or, at the very least, to keep my options open for university. I remember one of my sisters saying to me, 'Why aren't you doing music for A level?' It hadn't occurred to me at the time, and I thought to myself what a good idea it was. At the same time, I was very interested in art, so I ended up choosing chemistry, art and design and music. It was a really good combination, but it meant that I would never go on to be a vet.

Nestled between my sisters! See how different we look now (page 84!)

Playing in my grandparents house

Next, I set my heart on studying art after I had finished my A levels. I looked around a lot of London art colleges and was all ready to pick one of them when at the last minute I thought: No, this is not me, I want to sing. And so I did that instead.

I was a really disruptive child when I was younger. I had bad behavioural problems and that's why I think that when I was eight years old, my parents thought: Right … change of direction. Let's get him into music. This might sort him out.

The first musical thing I remember was when I was eight years old, when I started at Reigate St Mary's. It was a fairly small school with about two hundred and fifty pupils, of which fourteen were choristers. It was fantastic fun under the direction of my first singing teacher, Charles Thompson. I'm still in contact with him now all these years later and he's been very supportive of what I'm doing as part of G4. He really taught me the basics and discipline of singing. It was hard work: we sung five services a week and I did that every term-time week from the age of eight to thirteen. One of my proudest moments at the school was when I eventually became head chorister. Being there really set me up – not just vocally, but mentally. It was an excellent training and it gave me a professional attitude towards singing that has stayed with me ever since.

As a choir, we had fantastic opportunities, singing in films and on soundtracks. We were in *Four Weddings and a Funeral* as the choir in a couple of

the weddings and we did soundtrack work for films such as *The Browning Version* and some other lesser-known movies. It was brilliant fun for all of us.

Away from the more glitzy stuff that we did, the standard of singing in the choir was very high and I was being asked to do more and more solos once I had become head chorister. When my voice broke, I suddenly thought: I can't be bothered doing that any more. I didn't want to sing. In fact, I hated singing and I don't know to this day why I took it up again.

My senior school, Ardingly College, was very musical, although the music scholarship I had was for playing the flute rather than for doing anything vocal.

I started playing the piano instead of singing and, in the end, it was the flute that lost out, as I stopped playing that to start my singing again. I have never regretted it!

By the time I was doing my A levels the opportunities for musical performance were amazingly good. There was a large choral society and a very impressive orchestra. When we put the choir and the orchestra together on stage, it made a formidable sound. I got a real kick from performing even at that age and I particularly loved singing solo parts in oratorios with the full orchestra and choir. I was lucky

enough to get a great reception from people who heard me sing, which encouraged me even further.

I also played the timpani, or kettledrums, in the orchestra, which was great fun. Some people think that timpanists just whack a drum at the back of the stage, but actually they can control the whole dynamic of the orchestra. Whenever there was a bass solo to be sung in a concert, I would play in the timps section until I was due to sing, at which point, I would literally walk around the rest of the orchestra while they were still playing, to get into my singing position at the front of the stage.

In 1997, we performed at the Royal Albert Hall as part of a massed schools orchestra and choral concert. Instead of being in the choir, I was chosen to play percussion, mainly the timps and the triangle. Although it is not the noisiest of instruments, I was surprised, but I guess thrilled, when my music teacher told me afterwards that my triangle playing was fantastic. At the other end of the noise scale, I also played the cymbals during the national anthem, which was a bit of a buzz considering that Prince Edward was there as the royal family's representative. As soon as they hear a cymbal playing on stage in a concert, the audience looks straight at the person playing it and there is no hiding place if he or she makes a mistake. Luckily, I got it right on the night.

I've still never travelled outside Europe. For our family holidays, we always went to either the south of

France or around England. My parents are big fans of hiring a house or a cottage for us all to get together for a couple of weeks. Now that the three children have left home, we still try to get back together regularly and often use our trips away to visit family friends around England and Wales.

For many years, my sisters were always taller than me. Suddenly though, I shot up as a teenager and it became a real turning point for me when I was bigger and stronger than them. It's funny because when you are growing up and you have older sisters, they are always talking about their 'little brother'. But now, rather than me asking them for advice, they

now get advice from me and our relationships have totally changed. It is a shame that Amy and her husband Marcus live down in Devon because it is a bit too far away, but we still see each other as often as we can. My parents are both only children, so I do not have any aunts, uncles or cousins. I think it makes us a far stronger family unit. We are a really close-knit group and I know how lucky we are to have a mum and dad who are still very happy together after thirty years of marriage.

It has been really important to me to have had a strong circle of family and friends around me during the first year of G4. I cannot imagine having done it without them, to be honest. There are so many people that get to the top and then mess themselves up. It is one thing to go out on stage and have people love you, but when the applause dies away and you are backstage, or on your own driving home, or just going about doing normal everyday things, you need to have support behind you or else I think it would be very hard to cope with it all. Perhaps that lack of support is why some people in the public spotlight plainly don't cope.

When it came to leaving school and going on to university, some of my teachers were a little apprehensive about the possibility of me going to music college. I was advised that perhaps it was a little risky and that maybe I should go away to university and study for a degree in another subject, before returning to study singing later on. At the time, many of the people starting the undergraduate courses at music colleges were as old as 23 or 24. I had been given a consultation at the Guildhall School of Music and Drama when I was about sixteen, where the teachers listen to you and advise you on whether you should consider coming back for a full audition when you're older. I had been given a positive response and they told me I had potential. In the end, I auditioned and found that I was by no means the youngest in the class. It's a funny thing with music college that if they see a spark in you when you audition, they tend to offer you a place because the tutors know that if they delay, another music college will take you on. In London, there are several colleges competing for students.

I decided to take a gap year after my A levels. I know that people use this as an opportunity to travel the world, but I didn't do anything exotic. Instead, I worked full-time to save up for London as a porter at Effingham Park Hotel in Surrey. It was a really good experience and it made me appreciate people who work full time and do a proper nine-to-five job – although my hours there were on shifts, so were anything but nine to five. It was a really interesting experience and gave me an insight into how the place worked. At that stage, I had never stayed in a hotel myself, instead just seeing them as swanky places for other people.

My mum instilled into me the need to work hard in the job because the hotel management would, in the future, be able to provide me with a reference for any other work I did after university. She told me that if I didn't do well there, I might have trouble getting employment elsewhere.

I took Mum's advice to heart and was really careful and conscientious about everything. I always made sure that I dressed smartly and worked really hard.

Just as I was about to leave, the boss said, 'It's a shame you're going because you've got the potential to make head porter.' Even though I knew that I didn't want to work in a hotel as a full-time career, it gave me a lot of satisfaction that it had been a job well done.

My first two years at the Guildhall School of Music and Drama were great, but years three and four were even more enjoyable. It was the people around me who made it such a rewarding place to be. A university or college is only as good as the friends that you make while you are there. They have all stayed in contact and have been hugely supportive through all of our adventures as G4, as have the Guildhall, itself and its new principal, Barry Ife, and the Finance Department. It has been great to go back to visit the college, although it seems so long ago that we were there as students, even though we only actually graduated in the summer of 2004.

All my singing teachers at the Guildhall helped me in different ways. Jane Highfield gave me a lot of confidence to perform and Brian Parsons persuaded me to sing out and have fun. But then I had some vocal problems and John Evans helped me to see the light at the end of the tunnel. Everything I had learned in the past suddenly seemed to make sense, thanks to his teaching.

My musical heroes include classical artists such as the Welsh bass baritone Bryn Terfel and the American soprano Renèe Fleming. I always wanted to be like Bryn when I was younger because his was the sort of voice that I dreamed of having. He was originally a Guildhall student and he came back when we were in our first year to sing the lead role in *Elijah*. It was a real privilege to be singing behind him in the chorus. I absolutely adore Renèe's voice and I was lucky enough to hear her singing at the Barbican concert hall in London. When she sang a high note, it was like being in a cocoon and I felt completely immersed in it. She has such a fantastic, huge voice and I would recommend her or Bryn's CDs to anyone who is keen to learn more about opera.

The work I did at the Guildhall was a very good grounding, but moving from the classical-music world into the pop-music world meant that that I had lots to learn.

Everything about classical music is about live performance – what you see, is what you get. In the pop world, the accent is placed far more upon heavy production.

The danger is that because everything is made to be so perfect in the studio, it can be hard for acts to replicate the sound they make when they sing live. We pride ourselves on our live vocal performances. Many of our fans say to us that they now listen to more classical music than they used to because they have heard us singing classical tracks. And that is something that I am really happy about achieving as a by-product of our success in the pop charts.

NAME:	Jonathan Ansell.
VOICE:	Tenor.
BIRTHDAY:	10 March 1982.
STAR SIGN:	Pisces.
BORN:	Carshalton, Surrey.
MUSICAL INSTRUMENTS:	Trumpet (Grade 5), Violin (Grade 3), Piano (odd note).
MUSICAL INFLUENCES:	Mozart, the Three Tenors, Andrew Lloyd Webber and Queen.
ALL-TIME GREATEST MUSICIAN:	Luciano Pavarotti.
WOULD MOST LIKE TO PERFORM WITH:	Queen – they are just legends.
IDEAL WOMAN:	Petite, cute face, good laugh and nice smile.
FAVOURITE FOOD:	Ice cream.
FAVOURITE BOOK:	*Kestrel for a Knave* by Barry Hines.
FAVOURITE FILM:	*Willie Wonka & the Chocolate Factory*.
FAVOURITE WAY TO RELAX:	Being outside – driving, fishing and power kiting.
FOOTBALL CLUB:	I've never been into football.
DREAM HOLIDAY DESTINATION:	Barbados – or even the moon. Now that would be cool!
MOST ANNOYING HABIT:	Chewing the insides of my cheeks.
MOST OVERUSED WORD:	Cool.
JOB IF NOT IN MUSIC:	Managing a successful company.
WORST G4 MOMENT:	The boot camp stage of *The X-Factor*.
BEST G4 MOMENT:	Performing in the Royal Albert Hall in London on our tour.
THE REST OF G4 SAY:	'Jon's incessantly tidy, so when he lived in the same flat as Ben, who is incredibly messy, for eight weeks, it was a complete nightmare.'

Jon's Story

WHEN I was a kid, I lived with my family in a three-bedroom terrace house not far from where I was born in Carshalton in Surrey. Our home backed on to a common with a big hill where we would play in the snow in winter.

My brother Christopher is three years older and my sister Jennifer is five years younger than me. She would prefer it if I called her Jenny as everyone else does, but she's always been Jennifer to me, so she's going to be Jennifer in our book. Jennifer had her own room and Christopher and I shared a room, sleeping in bunk beds.

My dad, Brian, worked at Surrey University, teaching on a science roadshow that toured schools. Then he went into classroom teaching, specialising first in physics and then in design technology, before going back to the sciences and maths. Now, he's the manager of an adult education centre.

My mum, Pauline, is a primary school teacher. She looks after the music side of things in her school, running the choir and teaching the recorder to all of the kids. She manages to get the best out of the children and I think that it's really important that young kids have the opportunity to take part in music at school. I was lucky in that I was given those opportunities. Very quickly, I found how much I loved making music. It was never something that I was

forced to do by my mum and dad and, because the choice about whether I did it was mine, it has probably helped to build my passion for music over the years that have followed.

My family is really important to me. When you are younger, you do go through a period when you're trying to get away from them, but then you realise the importance of these people to you. Mum and Dad have always been incredibly strong for all of us. I know that I was a pain in the neck when I was a kid – very annoying and a real little tearaway. I loved getting into mischief.

When we were younger, my parents had long summer breaks, so we went on a series of Eurocamp holidays.

The drive down to France would last for way too long, as we were rammed into the back of our trusty red Vauxhall Cavalier.

Above our heads, the roof rack was piled high with all the gear we would need for our time away. There was only a certain amount of space into which we could squeeze our legs, because there was so much crammed into the back of the car. We used to have to take off our shoes so that we could fit our feet into the gaps that Dad had carefully crafted.

After what seemed like days of travelling, we

would eventually arrive feeling tired, but excited. These trips were always really lovely and I have some very happy memories, although sometimes it rained torrentially and we had to dig trenches around our tent to stop ourselves from being washed away.

As a boy, alongside music, my other great passion in life was the great outdoors and it is something that has stayed with me ever since. I was in both the Cubs and the Scouts and loved going away to camp, enjoying all the rituals involved with gathering and chopping wood and making the camp fire. When I was older, I went on to do the Gold Duke of Edinburgh's Award and, once again, I loved the experience of being outdoors. To qualify for the award, I walked a stupid amount of miles in Snowdonia together with a group of friends. It was

only later that I found out that glandular fever was kicking in and I ended up being knocked out of school for a whole term. I was quite fit and active at the time, but I began to feel odd while we were on the walk, suddenly becoming very tired. Despite not feeling great, getting my Gold Award was an amazing achievement and I collected it from Buckingham Palace at the same time as Christopher picked up his.

I had a great passion for fishing and I still sneak off with my rod and some bait whenever I can, although it's one of the things that I don't seem to have as much time for since G4 really took off. I love going down to the water and often don't really catch anything very much. But that doesn't stop me from sitting there for hours, trying. The attraction for me is being away from everything and being able to just sit

silly faces while driving away from X-Factor show

Top of Snowdon as part of Gold Duke of Edinburgh Award

Tom, Nick and I being Chippendales for fancy dress

Summer holiday in Canary Islands 2005

there and think. I always need my quiet time, even now. My parents tend to worry when I go fishing because they think there must be something wrong. That's probably because when some mad change is happening in my life, I tend to disappear off to a beach or a riverbank in search of some solitude, so that I can get everything into perspective. Some people get hideously drunk, but I go fishing. I know it sounds weird – but it's my escape. I'm at one with nature, which might be a cliché, but it really does feel like that to me. If I catch something, then it's wicked, but if I don't, then I have still had the chance to sit there and chill out.

If I catch something from the sea, it's great to be able to take it home and lay out the fish on the kitchen table, before feeding them to the family. I

was never as good at freshwater fishing – everything was too small and fiddly and I have always had much more luck with sea fishing.

I really love going spinning for bass, which is a type of fishing that most people have never heard about. I get up at around three o'clock in the morning and go straight down to the beach. The sea is completely calm, it's virtually dark and the sun is just about to come over the horizon. I wade out in my swimming shorts. All around me, fish are jumping out of the water, birds are diving in and sometimes a whole shoal of mackerel might swim past. Even if I don't catch anything, it's a beautiful experience to be right in there amongst nature.

These days I do enjoy going out clubbing with my friends, but that's the way I relax if there isn't a lot of time available to me. If I do have more time though, I much prefer to drive down to Bognor and walk along the seafront, with friends or family, or even on my own. Then, if I get the chance to grab a rod and to go out fishing, I find that the ultimate way of chilling. If I was unable to escape by doing this sort of thing every so often, then I would just implode.

I want to charter a whole boat and invite all of my friends down for a day's fishing. Up until now, I have always been on charter trips where you pay thirty pounds for a day, but you find yourself with a load of people who you don't know. It would be lovely to have the whole boat and to be able to ask the skipper to go exactly where I wanted to go. Buying a boat for myself, a few years down the line, is an incredible dream of mine.

At school, I was a bit of a terror, but music somehow just got me. Having the opportunity to sing unleashed the good side of me. I spent more time out of the classroom than I did inside when I was in language classes. I always answered back to the teachers and I tended to be a little bit too cocky for my own good. I hope that I've now learned how to channel that in a humorous way. I found lots of school very difficult, especially when things were written down. It was only years later, when I went to university, that I found out I had dyslexia. I didn't know about it through all of my schooling, so everyone thought that I simply had a very short attention span. In truth, I tried to pay attention for as

long as I could, but then a switch would click in my head and I always found my mind drifting.

If we were in class taking part in a group discussion then it was fine, but as soon as we were asked to write anything down, I started to have problems. Everything would whizz around my brain and I knew what I thought about what was going on. I just had trouble processing those thoughts on to paper, which meant that I would then get frustrated with myself and would use cockiness to diffuse the situation.

My love of music started at a family party one Christmas when I asked if I could sing to everyone. I have no idea where it came from. The first song that I really remember is 'Love Changes Everything', which was a hit for Michael Ball, and came from the Andrew Lloyd Webber musical *Aspects of Love*.

For some reason, I used to sing it all over the place. Once, I was standing next to Christopher in the queue to go swimming at a leisure centre and I started belting it out, much to his embarrassment.

I honestly could not tell you what first inspired me to burst into song, but once I started, I have not stopped since.

Going to church on Sundays was quite important to me when I was younger. There was always a lovely atmosphere and I enjoyed taking part in the musical side of things. I have drifted away from it now, but I do think that everyone should try to lead a good life within the community with their friends and family. In a few years time, I will probably end up going back to church more regularly. It can be difficult because sometimes people are looked down upon for being over-religious. I wouldn't say that I am extremely devout, but I would never criticise anyone for practising the religion they believe in.

Having a set of beliefs certainly gives you a grounding from an early age, which helps you to live your life later on. It's a sort of moral compass against which you can make your decisions. I have become ever more grateful for that grounding and I believe that it has played a big part in making me the person I am today. I don't sit and pray every night, but I must admit that when we were waiting for the results on *The X-Factor*, I did send up the odd word. Unfortunately, I suppose that is the way religion works for some people: we tend to buy into it when we want something, rather than when we are giving something back, which is a shame.

The music in my life stemmed from my early years at church and then from school. I was lucky enough in my primary school to play the title role in a production of Andrew Lloyd Webber's and Tim Rice's musical *Joseph and the Amazing Technicolor Dreamcoat*. Some of the teachers were worried that if I played such a big part, my marks would go down because I would be focusing too much on the role,

but actually it went the other way. It was the first indication that even though music was taking up my time, my personal fulfilment from performing helped me academically.

I joined the West Sussex Boys Choir at the age of seven and a half with a conductor called Arthur Robson and a lady called Eileen Burrows, who accompanied us. The choir was basically made up of a load of mates. We would rehearse every couple of weeks and would get a real buzz from performing in our concerts. In the breaks, we would mess around, before getting back to the singing again. There was a real contrast in how we behaved outside, kicking the hell out of each other on the rugby field, before coming in and singing 'In Paridisum'. We looked and sounded so angelic with our unbroken voices, but then shortly afterwards, we'd be back outside, beating each other up in the playground.

Some people think that if you take part in classical singing, you must be boring and pompous, which is absolute rubbish.

We were just normal kids doing all the normal things that other boys of our age were doing. The only difference was that we got a thrill out of singing beautiful music.

I took part in a tour of Florida when I was eleven and we also toured in Europe, so I had some fantastic opportunities to travel. When we performed

at the National Youth Music Festival at the Royal Festival Hall in London, I was lucky enough to sing the solo 'Panis Angelicus'. It was at the time when *The Choir* was on television and that particular song was the big classical music anthem of the moment.

I was incredibly nervous about giving that performance and I became so worked up that I was physically sick the night before and on the coach journey up to London. It was horrific because I knew that London was a massive place and in my mind I had pictured a huge audience. When we arrived, I discovered that the audience was in fact only made up of a panel of judges and the family and friends who had come up with us in the coach. So, all of that worry and angst was for nothing.

It sounds really stupid now, but I had panic attacks for a long time as a boy when I sung in public. I used to wake up with the sensation that I was upside down, which sounds absolutely ridiculous. I know that it doesn't make sense when you think of what that actually means, but that's what I felt like when I was younger. One time, when I had woken up with the feeling in the middle of the night, my dad tucked me back in bed with my feet on the pillow and I felt better. Eventually, I grew out of it and became far more comfortable performing in public. Now that I am singing with G4, I tend to feel a surge of excitement when I walk out on stage rather than nerves.

I played the violin and trumpet as a youngster, but I never felt the same passion for them as I did for singing. I got my Grade 8 singing at the age of thirteen as a treble, which is very young. I was determined to pass the exam as a singer because I

was worried that I would miss the opportunity if my voice broke and I was no longer able to sing well afterwards. My voice didn't officially break until I was sixteen, which was quite late. From the age of fourteen onwards, I went for singing lessons after school with a guy called Martin Eliott. At first I had lessons as a treble, but then as my voice deepened, I started to learn about singing as a tenor. It was odd because I was still using my boyish voice to sing in the West Sussex Boys Choir. Eventually, I had to call it a day in the choir, which was a sad moment because I had been a member for eight-and-a-half years. After my voice broke, I didn't stop singing, but it did become weaker for a short period while I settled down into being a tenor.

I was also doing my GCSEs at the time and singing in a boys' choir wasn't necessarily the coolest thing to be doing. When you are really young, people think it is cute, but when you still do it in your teenage years, the ridicule from some of your school colleagues can be quite tough.

I enjoyed secondary school, especially at the stage where I could pick my subjects for A level. I chose physics, music and design and technology. I dropped the physics after a year because unfortunately, although I loved the processes and the concepts, once the equations had to be worked out on paper, it went beyond me and I couldn't cope. I'm still fascinated by all sorts of topics within physics, geography and the natural world. I always want to know what makes this happen or why that works. It's something I must have inherited from my dad.

I obviously carried on with the music, but I also

continued with the design and technology. Today, I still have a table in my flat that I made for my A-level course. I was most proud of the legs because I had to bond and then turn the wood. My teachers thought that there was a chance it would rupture, but it held. I spent ages making sure that all the legs were exactly the same shape.

I carried on singing through my A levels with Martin Eliott as my teacher. My local MP, Howard Flight, heard me sing at a concert when I was seventeen and was so impressed that he arranged for me to go for a provisional audition at the Guildhall School of Music and Drama in London. I was unsure that I would be the right sort of material for them, but the tutors said, 'Yes, definitely come back and try out again for us next year.'

I ended up missing the audition twelve months later because of my glandular fever, but the college moved my session back a few months for me. My voice had just started to recover and I got through. They even ended up giving me a scholarship.

When I arrived in London, it was both scary and exciting to be starting a new life as a music student. At the time, I had a long-term girlfriend and I used to go home to see her and my family every weekend, so I didn't play as much of a part in the student life as I could have done initially, but I made up for it in the second and third years. That was a bit of a mad time for me, when perhaps I wasn't as focused on my singing as much as I should have been. It was good to get it out of my system though and I knuckled down to some hard work in the final year.

It is inevitable that everybody compares themselves to everybody else as performers at music college. It can be a very competitive environment and if you're going to achieve as an artist, you need to have a certain element of self-belief. You don't necessarily need to voice that self-belief to other people, but inwardly you need to have that drive and the knowledge that you can do what is required of you. Maybe you can't do it right now, or even next week, but in a few years' time, you know that you're going to be able to sing that aria. You have to set yourself new goals all of the time and then work towards them.

Many of the voices I worked alongside at the Guildhall were just phenomenal. I quickly realised that they were comparable to some of the albums I had listened to in the past and I felt that just getting the chance to sing with these people was great. I was also really lucky to be able to work with the best singing teacher I have ever had, Adrian Thompson. He has done amazing things to my voice.

Although I did a lot of training as an opera singer, I must admit that I always find it weird performing a role in an opera. It is nowhere near as rewarding as standing on the stage and being ourselves, doing our own interpretation of a song, as we have the opportunity to do now. Being in G4, we don't have to hide behind a role or a character, which makes singing even more exciting.

I am particularly proud of the way that, as G4, we have been able to seamlessly fuse together different genres of music into what we do. The human voice is a far more diverse instrument than people realise and we like to make sure that we give ours a challenging workout with the songs we perform and the style in which we sing them.

NAME:	Matthew William Tansley Stiff.
VOICE:	Bass/Baritone.
BIRTHDAY:	13 December 1979.
STAR SIGN:	Sagittarius.
BORN:	Grimsby.
MUSICAL INSTRUMENTS:	Bass trombone and guitar.
MUSICAL INFLUENCES:	Mozart, Oasis, rock and pop from the 60s, 70s, 80s and 90s.
ALL-TIME GREATEST MUSICIAN:	John Lennon and Paul McCartney.
WOULD MOST LIKE TO PERFORM WITH:	Queen – the greatest rock band ever.
IDEAL WOMAN:	Angelina Jolie.
FAVOURITE FOOD:	German salami.
FAVOURITE BOOK:	Anything by Terry Pratchett.
FAVOURITE FILM:	*Robin Hood: Prince of Thieves*.
FAVOURITE WAY TO RELAX:	Socialising with friends.
FOOTBALL CLUB:	Livingston.
DREAM HOLIDAY DESTINATION:	Cuba.
MOST ANNOYING HABIT:	I bite my nails.
MOST OVERUSED WORD:	'Y' know'.
JOB IF NOT IN MUSIC:	Book publisher.
WORST G4 MOMENT:	Any day we have to get up early in the morning – and there are a lot of them.
BEST G4 MOMENT:	Singing 'New York, New York' on the stage of the Royal Albert Hall to a packed house. Also, any day where we don't have to get up early in the morning.
THE REST OF G4 SAY:	'Matt's got an encyclopaedic knowledge of pop music. But then, because he's the oldest in the group, he was probably there when most of it was being done the first time around.'

Matt's Story

I 'M the only member of the group to have been born in the 1970s, although I managed to squeeze into that decade by just a couple of weeks. My dad worked for BT, as he still does today, and my mum was an officer in a children's home. She gave up work to have me, but is now a teaching assistant in a primary school. Now, it's not that I was unplanned, but it would be true to say that I came into the world a little bit sooner than they expected.

My brother Gareth is two years younger than me. We were lucky enough to have had a really good family life with a great relationship with Mum and Dad. On my mum's side, my grandma and grandad have always been very supportive, as has my nana on my dad's side. Tragically, my grandad passed away from throat cancer a few years ago, which was a terribly sad time for all of us.

Gareth and I were less close through our teenage years because he fulfilled the role of being my annoying little brother and it is only just recently that we have realised we are closer than we ever could have imagined.

My infant and junior school was about a ten-minute walk from our house in Grimsby and when I was really young I used to ride there on my tricycle, with my mum pushing me from behind. I don't remember it myself, but I am often reminded about my first day at school. I had spent the first five years of my life with my mother, I arrived at the gates of a big, unfamiliar building and then she turned around and walked away from me. Apparently, I started bawling my eyes out. Mum says that it was absolutely heartbreaking for her, but it is something

that every parent and child has to go through.

Once I got to school, I loved it. Thinking back, it seems such a long time ago now, but I had a very happy time there. I was a pretty good kid and was probably better behaved than the rest of the G4 boys. I can still remember all of my primary school teachers' names and it has struck me since what an impact on your life having a great teacher at that age can have.

At junior school, when I was knocking on for seven or eight, I formed a really close group of friends. It was about that time that I acquired the nickname 'Stiffy'. I was known as Stiffy right the way through my schooling and some of my best friends from home and university still call me it now. It has just been who I am. In fact, it only really changed when I went to the Guildhall School of Music and Drama to do my postgraduate course.

My parents still call me Matthew and my mum often says to me, 'Oh, you're not a Matt. You're a Matthew.' Having said that, she used to call me Stiffy as well during my teenage years. I was never a troublesome teenager, but sometimes I completely failed to register the word Matthew as being my name, because I was being called Stiffy by everyone else.

At secondary school, I was in the top two sets for every subject. I kept my head down and got my work done. I had a good group of friends, most of whom had moved up with me from primary to secondary school. I used to play Sunday football, usually as a defender, but as I became older, my musical commitments became pretty hefty and I played

me with my grandad

Ready for school

football less and less.

My musical career began when I was about eight years old. I did something called the Bentley Test, which helps teachers to assess a child's pitch, rhythm and tone. Apparently, I scored quite high and the teachers asked me if I would like to play a musical instrument.

'Yeah, OK,' I replied. After all, I was eight years old and I didn't have much else to do.

'How about a violin?' I was asked.

'No. That's a girl's instrument,' were the first words out of my mouth.

'OK. How about a brass instrument?'

'Yeah. I'd love to play the saxophone,' I replied, not knowing that the saxophone is actually a member of the woodwind family. The brass teacher, Evelyn Dawson, opened the instrument cupboard and I tried out the trumpet, French horn, euphonium, tuba and trombone. Often children are matched up to a brass instrument because of the shape of their mouths and mine seemed to fit the trombone best. This was in the good old days when musical-instrument lessons were free of charge for everyone. I was given the instrument and, on the way home, I bought my first music book for about £3.50. I was officially learning the trombone.

me and my brother

Early performance practice

I kept on studying it for the next three years – the rest of my time at primary school. Then my mum and dad bought me my first trombone of my own, a nickel-plated Besson, Boosey & Hawkes Series 600. At secondary school, I was taught by a local guy called Anthony Hall, who had studied at the Welsh College of Music and Drama. I kept on studying through the grades right up to Grade 8, when I specialised in the bass trombone.

When I was just a teenager, we went to see the Kingsway Printers Cleethorpes Band in a pub called the Spider's Web. It was a 25-piece brass band and was part of the huge Yorkshire tradition of

generations of great brass band music. I really enjoyed listening to them because they weren't just playing traditional music. They were also doing other pieces, such as 'New York, New York' and even 'The Stripper' and 'The Can-Can'.

After the show, we stayed behind to talk to the players and I told them about me and the trombone. They said that they rehearsed on Wednesdays and Sundays and invited me along. I ended up sitting in their rehearsal the following weekend in the bass trombone chair, joining in with the rest of the band where I could. I stayed with them for the best part of four years. I was lucky enough that one of the much

older guys, Eric Barnes, took me under his wing. He taught me a lot and I was always fascinated to hear the colourful stories he had to tell about his life. When he moved to the Market Rasen Band, I followed him. We used to rehearse at the racecourse and paid our rent by playing at the races on Saturdays.

At that point, I thought that the trombone was going to be what I would end up doing for a living. I had come to that decision despite the fact that my mum and dad were told by a teacher at a parents' evening that I probably should not take GCSE music because I would never make it as a musician. My mum still likes to remind me of this today!

I ignored the teacher and took GCSE music. When it came to the crunch, I decided to move onto do A levels at the local sixth-form college because I wanted to continue studying music.

It was a bit of a wrench leaving behind some of my friends from secondary school, but I had an absolutely brilliant time at Franklin College, so it was worth it. The music department had its own little section of the college, which for some reason was even kitted out with its own shower. David and Gill Parker taught the main music lessons and Anthony Hall continued to give me instrumental lessons. When he moved away, his uncle, Dr John Hall, a legend in the trombone world and a great teacher, looked after me for my final year there.

The team became such good friends and we were all like a happy family. It was a brilliant time and a great laugh. As well as studying music, I managed to fit in A levels in psychology and English literature and an AS level in philosophy and cultural beliefs. We used to have a long period for lunch on Thursdays, with music history not starting until three o'clock. Sometimes, we would get into my mate Adrian's car and drive down to Grimsby seafront. He would have a shandy while the rest of us knocked back three pints. We would play a few games of pool, before munching our way through a bag of fish and chips. We were never drunk, but it would be true to say that there would be a quarter-to-three haze when we arrived back in college. Music history always seemed to go a lot faster when we had been on one of those trips!

By now, I was also playing in the Grimsby and Cleethorpes District Youth Orchestra, or the GCDYO, as it is known to everyone. Some of my friends used to gently poke fun at me when I turned down invitations to play football because of band rehearsals. My weeks were busy: Youth Swing Band was on Monday nights and Cleethorpes Brass Band was on Tuesdays; rehearsals for the Concert Band at college happened on Wednesday afternoons, followed by Market Rasen that evening; Thursday was my night off, before a big session with the GCDYO on Fridays, with the first hour and a half being taken up by wind band and the second hour and a half by full orchestral practice.

Just after I had started studying for my music A level, Gill Parker said to me and two of my mates: 'You might need a second instrument to make it a bit easier to pass the course, so have you thought about singing?'

'You've got to be kidding,' we replied, 'we're all

brass players, for God's sake.' In the end, we decided to give it a go, just for a laugh. So all three of us went for a half-hour session to assess where we were. It was a bit of a giggle as far as we were concerned.

A few days later, Gill came up to me and said, 'Would you come on your own next week?'

'Why? What have I done?' I asked.

'Nothing. I'd just like to hear you on your own,' she said.

So I went along and started to have a forty-minute session every week. It was October 1996 and just six months later, in March 1997, I had passed my Grade 8 in singing. Bearing in mind that on trombone I had begun lessons at the age of eight and it had taken me nine years to reach that level, I was gobsmacked. It was even more surprising to find out that I had been awarded a merit for my singing exam. From that moment onwards, I never really looked back.

The first time I sung in public was at Easter in 1997, when the college put on Johann Sebastian Bach's *St Matthew Passion* at St James's church in Grimsby. They split the songs up between all the different soloists in the college. Most people would never dream of tackling this work until they had been singing for a good five years – we had no fear though. We thought we were the bees' knees. In fact, I was a complete infant when it came to vocal music and I didn't really know much of the repertoire. In that particular concert, I was in the choir as well as singing solo. Even though nowhere near all of the notes were right, it was one of those great moments of relief when we finally went off stage. I had been so nervous beforehand and, once I had finished my solo, I had to walk back in front of the orchestra to rejoin

the chorus. I remember thinking that I was going to collapse because a shooting pain went down the nerves in the back of my leg. For a moment, I thought that somebody had kicked me, but then I realised it was because of the amount of tension I was feeling.

These days, I don't get anywhere near as nervous as I used to. I think that you learn over the years to channel that nervous energy to your advantage.

Music teachers are fantastic people and I owe a lot to Gill Parker. Recently, I mentioned her when we fronted the Classic FM Music Teacher of the Year competition. She sent me a text saying that she had heard me talking about how brilliant she was on the radio but, had it not been for her asking me to have a singing lesson and then for the way in which she taught me so much, I would never have come close to playing my part in G4's success today.

Another defining moment in my life came when I took the decision about what I was going to study at university. For a long time, I thought I would do psychology as a career because it interested me and I could see that it could help me to end up in a well-paid job. People intrigued me and I became fascinated with the power of the mind and mental health. Coupled with that, I was very interested in philosophy and the big questions of life. It's amazing how the mind works: how easily it can be tricked and how we can get so many things wrong and yet store up so much information.

I was dead set on studying the subject at university and it was not until two months before I actually took my A levels that I sat down and thought that studying psychology might be a waste of what was, at that point, ten years of musical training.

So I changed my mind. I was going to stay at college for another year to study A-level music technology because I was very interested in the recording and computer programming side of music. But on A-level results day, I was sitting at home celebrating with a good mate called Peter Simons, who was going to Huddersfield University to study music. He suggested that I give them a ring to see if there were any spare places on the course. So I decided to give it a go.

They called me back and invited me along for an audition. The admissions tutor said on the phone, 'I see from your application that you're a trombone player?' I was sitting in the hallway at home and, to this day I don't know why, but I replied: 'Yes, I play the trombone, but I'd like to come to you to study as a singer.' I do not know for the life of me why I did that. I had been playing trombone for ten years and had been singing for just eighteen months, but because I had achieved my Grade 8 in both, I was free to choose which one I carried on with.

Getting into Huddersfield was all based on how I did in an audition. So I went along and sang a few pieces to one of the music teachers. Afterwards, I sat around the table with my parents and the admissions tutor, Michael Holloway. He turned to me and said, 'If we offered you a place, would you accept it?'

I looked across the table at my mum and she said, 'If you want to?'

'Yeah, go on then,' I replied.

Within three weeks, I had packed up and was living in a university hall of residence in Huddersfield.

I had become a music student. Little did I know that not only would I be there for three years doing my first degree, I would also stay for an extra year to study for an MA in Musical Performance.

At Huddersfield, I encountered a whole host of new people and my four years there were absolutely brilliant. I met my best friends through university and I'm still close to most of them today. The social side of the music department was brilliant. As soon as I got there, I became really good friends not just with people in my year, but also with guys in the second and third years. Everyone just mixed in together. We used to drink in a pub called the County in the centre of Huddersfield, just near the town hall. It still remains the best pub I've ever been to in my entire life. The highlight of the week was karaoke night on Wednesdays. We all turned out every week and I always did 'New York, New York' as my party piece. Amazingly, it was the song I sang as my solo on our first G4 tour in the summer of 2005. After we'd been to the County, we would go on to the Pepper House, a place of riotous drinking and debauchery.

The music department at Huddersfield has its own society, which has an elected committee of five. The common practice for someone who wanted to be president of the society was to put themselves forward at the end of the second year. It was not as serious as it sounds and was basically a popularity contest. I was persuaded to stand for the presidency at the end of my first year against three other people. I managed to come second, but twelve months later I stood again and won. My old mate Peter Simons, who had persuaded me to go to Huddersfield in the first place, was my vice-president. The committee's job was to organise parties for the students throughout the year and run a small shop in the music department. All profit went towards the summer ball.

It was in my second year at Huddersfield that I met Amy, who is now my girlfriend. We have been together throughout my time in G4, which has been quite strange. It can be tough on her because we don't always see a lot of each other. Being in a band, you don't exactly lead a conventional nine-to-five life. But we are getting used to it now and she has always been hugely supportive of me.

Becoming a professional singer is not something I really thought about doing, I just did music because I enjoyed it. So after my first degree ended, it seemed logical to carry on and do the MA at Huddersfield under the guidance of my singing teacher at the time, Paul Wade.

After that finished, I moved back home to Grimsby and had a year out. I did some work in the chorus of Opera North, but I was on the dole four times. I used to walk into the dole office on Freeman Street in Grimsby and I see people there who did not have anywhere near the opportunities that I have been given. I am very fortunate not to have experienced being unemployed for long periods, but I have been there.

I remember something my grandad said to me after my GCSEs, when I went to work in a fresh-fish factory in Grimsby during my summer holidays. I began on the lines, putting salmon into vacuum packs. It was mind-numbingly boring and I came home after the first week and asked my grandad, 'What am I doing this for?'

'You're doing this because you need the money and you're safe in the knowledge that you're not going to do it for the rest of your life. You're educating yourself and you're going to be doing something else. Put it into perspective: some people there have never had the opportunities that you have had. It doesn't mean that they're any less intelligent than you are – they just haven't had the opportunities. Just appreciate it for what it is. Do it, and then move on,' he very wisely told me.

I've taken those words with me because it's true that not everyone is as fortunate as me. I'm lucky enough to have been born into a loving family who didn't have loads of money by any stretch of the

imagination. But they made everything available to me and my brother. I had a good education and I managed to fund myself throughout. During my A levels, I worked for two years in a frozen-pea factory and, aside from the smell of the fresh fish, it was even worse than my previous summer job. I mean, peas – tons and tons of them pouring out of a chute. And it never stops. I did nights as well and that was really soul destroying. But I remembered Grandad's words.

So I ended up falling into a life of music because I enjoyed it. When I realised that I could make a living out of it, it just seemed the most natural thing to be doing. It was quite a practical decision. I feel quite balanced in the sense that I'm an instrumental musician, a singer and I'm also quite happy as the guy behind the scenes moving the stage blocks. I decided to study it further in London by doing a one-year master's degree in opera at the Guildhall School of Music and Drama. It was there that I met three guys, who were coming to the end of their undergraduate degree and who were looking for a bass to sing in their barbershop quartet. The rest, as they say, is history.

NAME:	Ben Thapa.
VOICE:	Tenor.
BIRTHDAY:	2 March 1982.
STAR SIGN:	Pisces.
BORN:	Cambridge.
MUSICAL INSTRUMENTS:	Clarinet.
MUSICAL INFLUENCES:	Luciano Pavarotti, Bryn Terfel and Thomas Allen.
ALL-TIME GREATEST MUSICIAN:	Mozart.
WOULD MOST LIKE TO PERFORM WITH:	Bond. They're great players and they *are* gorgeous!
IDEAL WOMAN:	Talkative, honest, genuine and caring, without hope or agenda…
FAVOURITE FOOD:	Sweet potatoes.
FAVOURITE BOOK:	*About a Boy* by Nick Hornby. I was gripped.
FAVOURITE FILM:	*Love Actually*. Dream the dream!
FAVOURITE WAY TO RELAX:	Clothes shopping. I love Ted Baker.
FOOTBALL CLUB:	Cambridge United. Save our club – they need your support!
DREAM HOLIDAY DESTINATION:	I've been to Canada and I loved it there.
MOST ANNOYING HABIT:	Channel surfing all the time on Sky Plus TV.
MOST OVERUSED WORD:	I say 'kinda' too much. I think the words 'unique' and 'exceptional' are way overused. And why when someone is hungry do they claim to be 'starving'?
WORST G4 MOMENT:	Jon losing his voice on *The X-Factor*. We were scared that we might not be able to perform.
BEST G4 MOMENT:	Singing on the Royal Albert Hall stage to a sell-out crowd.
THE REST OF G4 SAY:	'Ben is incredibly untidy and a bit scatter-brained sometimes. He's always leaving his mobile phone in the back of cabs and having to chase them down the road.'

Ben's Story

MY childhood was very different to the other guys in the band. My dad left when I was four years old. He came to Britain on a work visa and ended up being deported. That meant that I was raised by my mum up until the age of eleven. She was quite badly affected by my dad leaving and became ill. As a result of which I was fostered along with my sister, Beverley, who is eighteen months younger than me, and our brother, Bobby, who is eighteen months younger than her.

I am probably closest to Beverley out of everyone and she comes to see us perform whenever she can. She has been really supportive to me and it gives me an enormous amount of personal satisfaction to see how much enjoyment she also gets out of me being in the band. My brother is also reaping a few benefits of being related to somebody in G4. He turned up for a job interview and, because we have a reasonably uncommon surname, he was asked, 'Are you related to that guy from G4?'

'Yes,' he replied.

'Right, start Monday,' said his new boss.

Bobby and I used to squabble like anything when we were boys. I suppose that it always annoyed me that he was stronger than me, even though he was three years younger.

All three of us used to try to stay in contact with our dad in the years after he went abroad. When I had just turned twelve, he rang me up and said, 'Happy Birthday. I know it's been a difficult time. Have a really good day and I'll ring you next week.' That was the last time I have ever spoken to him. I suppose that we all thought that one day he was going to come back, but as I became old enough to form my own opinions, the gradual realisation dawned that he was never going to return. Knowing that I was unlikely to see him again was devastating at the time, but over the years since, it is something that I have come to terms with.

Because of my family situation, many of the opportunities that other people had during their childhood were never on offer for me. I think that helped me appreciate a lot more about what I was doing and really drove me onwards. I especially noticed the difference in my background to those people with classic two-parent family upbringings when I went to music college, which was a very

wondering if we are ever going to start rehearsals

with my classmates from Park Side Community college

private-school orientated environment. Not only was I from a state school, but I also had an unorthodox background. I tended not to mention it to a lot of people.

When I went into foster care at the age of eleven, I was told by some people that I would be doing really well if I managed to get myself a job, let alone go to university and have a career afterwards. I was incredibly keen to prove everyone wrong, saying 'I am going to do this.' I knew from when I was around fourteen years old that singing was something I wanted to take on to the next stage so that I could hopefully make a career out of it.

Back then, people advised me against concentrating too much on music because they said that so few musicians make it. I was constantly asked, 'Are you sure that this is what you want to do?' But that determination to prove people wrong has stood me in good stead. I can be so stubborn at times and it is a big part of who I am now, I guess, for good and for bad. When things go wrong, people often question whether they should give up and do something else, but I have never been a quitter. Even if something ultimately does not work out and I end up falling on my sword, I would rather do that than not have a go at it in the first place.

All of my experiences from my childhood have been integral to the person I have become. I know that when parents split up, it can really affect children, but it can be a very positive experience too. So many people patronise kids who have had unorthodox upbringings, but mine really has given me the strength to push forwards, learn and achieve.

Because I was independent from a young age, I learned to be a very private person. So, when I first started talking about my childhood background, I found it very difficult. It was a big thing for me to make something like that public. I really hope that it will encourage people who are facing difficulties in their lives not to give up because they see other people around them being given opportunities that they themselves do not have. If they carry on, they will achieve. I believe that there are so many gifted individuals who give up because they wrongly feel that they are a lesser person than those around them.

I grew up in Cambridgeshire and went to several different primary schools because we often moved house. It was only when I reached secondary school and I started being fostered that I stayed at one school for a long period of time. Parkside Community College was a massively stabilising influence on me in many ways. Looking back now, when I was very young, I was always scared of being a tough kid and when I was told off, it was a complete disaster in my life. Then I went completely the other way for a while. I was in care and I became really slapdash, not completing the schoolwork I was supposed to do and being very casual about things in general.

But then I did a lot of thinking about myself. And by the time I joined the sixth form I had managed to find both ways and reasons for doing what I wanted to do. Achieving good grades at school became really important to me. I decided that it would show

Age 6, with my sister and brother

On stage at The Royal Albert Hall

genuine strength of character if I could live independently, hold down a full-time job and still get good A-level grades.

My interest in music was there right the way through my childhood. It was sparked by one of my godmothers, Maggie, who has been a fantastic influence on my life. She is a Catholic and we used to go to church quite a lot from a young age. I started singing in a choir and, even though I was pretty awful when I was a boy, I used to really enjoy it. When my voice started breaking, I carried on going to church and enjoying the music. When I was fourteen, I started taking proper singing lessons there with my first singing teacher, Julia Caddick.

When you're a boy going through those early teen years, it's not necessarily the coolest thing to turn up and sing each week. It is definitely not the coolest thing in school to be a foster kid and I was pretty big as well, so I had a triple helping of bullying. Kids can be so cruel at that age and it was sheer bloody-mindedness on my part that made me determined to prove these people wrong. I always wondered what it was that the bullies got out of it all. Did it make them feel better? Was I just an easy target? One of the lovely things we have had along the way is hearing of more kids, particularly boys, joining choirs and generally singing since our times on *The X-Factor*. I think the more provision that can be made the better and if we can establish singing as a cool and fun pastime or hobby that would be a really fantastic thing to achieve.

Handel's *Messiah* is one of my earliest musical memories. I sang it a couple of times as a boy and it has lived with me ever since. We did performances of it when I was at college, where I had a solo role and

that was an incredible experience for me. As a piece of music, it has always had a deep emotional effect on me lifting up my spirits and giving me a sense of well-being and calm that can be hard to replicate in any other way. I will always link this piece to my childhood experiences and the way that music counselled me from such a young age.

When I started taking singing lessons, I discovered that I had perfect pitch. That means that whenever I hear a piece of music I can instantly recognise the musical key which it is in.

Since we joined together as G4 this has been especially useful because I know what note to give the guys whenever we start an a cappella track, so that we don't begin randomly. When we are arranging a piece, I can sit there and say, 'Oh, you sing that note and you sing that note.' It's definitely a useful tool to have.

The world of perfect pitch can sound a little strange to those people who don't have it. I read in a book somewhere that most loos flush in the key of E flat and I must admit that straight away afterwards I went to the bathroom to analyse whether my own toilet flushed in that key. Then there was a guy with perfect pitch who wrote to the BBC World Service to complain because the pips just before the news bulletin were in the key of C one day, rather than being in B flat, as usual. The reason was a technical fault that had ever so slightly speeded them up – and this is by an absolutely minute amount – which had made them change key. For me, that level of attention to perfect pitch is maybe a little on the excessive side! But it is true that I do go around sometimes thinking, 'Oh, that vacuum cleaner is in key, or that church bell is in the key of G' to the point where it is often a subject of humour amongst the group.

Musically, having perfect pitch can be something that holds you back if you are not careful. There are times when music can become way too considered and this can especially be the case if you have a tool like perfect pitch. You get so used to the idea of doing things exactly in tune that you can become frustrated when you hear even the slightest imperfection in a piece of music. When you hear a pop song and a note is slightly off you say 'ooh' to yourself because it seems so wrong, but once you realise that the flaw you can hear is deliberate, you understand that it's quite clever in that context. One of the most important things I have learned is to enjoy music at every level, whatever flaws there may be. As G4, we are all extremely fortunate to be earning a living doing what we love, but it is important that everyone has the opportunity to enjoy music, whatever their abilities.

My music carried on right through my teenage years and on more than one occasion it was a bit of an escape from some of the other things that were going on in my life. Once I had decided that I was going to live on my own from the age of sixteen, I needed to find myself a job so that I could afford to pay for a flat, food and clothes, while I studied for my A levels. The parents of Jeremy Jones, one of my friends at school, were the landlord and landlady of a pub called the Salisbury Arms, which is near the railway station in the centre of Cambridge. I worked at the Salisbury Arms in the kitchen from when I was sixteen and then graduated to bar work once I had turned eighteen. There is no getting away from the fact that it was hard work. I would go to college in the mornings followed by a lunch-time shift at the pub; then it was back to college in the afternoon with a full evening shift at the pub ending my day. I was also studying in my own time for my A levels. I needed to work for around forty hours a week to cover my living expenses. It was tough on occasions, but I loved it. Sadly, Jeremy's dad died of cancer last year and it is one of my lasting regrets that I was unable to attend his funeral due to filming commitments for *The X-Factor*. He and all the Jones family were a tremendous support at a difficult time in my life. Having that space of my own was a completely liberating experience.

Now, all four of us have just moved into new flats and I absolutely love living on my own again. It's so important for me to be able to close the door and have some private time. At first, when I was sixteen, it was hard because I was always used to having somebody else around. I lived on microwave meals initially, but eventually I learned how to do a few little bits for myself in the kitchen. It would be true to say that on some occasions I was envious of some aspects of the lives of my friends at sixth-form college, who would go home to their parents every night. I had a very different sort of life, but there is no doubt in my mind that it helped to mould me into the person I am today.

Living on my own taught me a lot about independence and fending for myself. I suppose that it's a little strange for me now being a part of G4, because there are four of us looking out for each other. At first, it was a little difficult for me to acclimatise to that, but now I love it.

I know that I have had a different upbringing from most people, but I am not sure that I would have developed the same ambition to succeed, had my childhood been more conventional. I believe that you have to embrace the gifts that you have been given and all the problems you face in life, whatever they

may be, are there for a reason. They have clearly shaped me as an individual.

After finishing my GCSEs at Parkside Community College, I went on to do my A levels at Hills Road Sixth-Form College in Cambridge. It had an amazing music department and a massive symphony orchestra. I played the clarinet and I will always be so grateful to them for giving me the opportunity to perform in such a great orchestra, especially considering I was such a shocking clarinet player. One of the highlights of each term was a large-scale orchestral and choral concert in Cambridge. One of my coolest memories is a tour of the Czech Republic during the upper sixth, when I was asked to perform solos with the orchestra and was given the opportunity to experience Europe for the first time.

These days, the extent and diversity of my music taste is ridiculous. In my CD racks I have everything from an entire collection of Mozart piano concertos through to Coldplay and the Scissor Sisters. When I drive around, I listen to my iPod. I have a huge range of tracks loaded onto it, from the Swedish tenor, Nicolai Gedda, through to Joss Stone and Kelly Clarkson. The guys always joke that I bought an iPod before I bought a computer – I suppose one example of foresight – some might call

me scatterbrain!'

Aside from music, cricket is the other big love of my life and I used to play in the college team. I always had visions that some day I would score a century for England in a test match. To be honest, I was a pretty average player, but I used to love taking part every Saturday and Sunday afternoon through the summer, not to mention practising in the wind and rain during the winter. Then, all of a sudden, the weekends became more filled with music. I remember the big choice came when I had choir rehearsals on a Thursday afternoon and I had to decide between singing or playing cricket for the college first team. I ended up missing a cricket cup final because I had to do my music. We lost the game by a handful of runs and I felt horrendously guilty.

My sixth-form college was quite academic and I was encouraged to apply for a choral scholarship to either Oxford or Cambridge universities. My teachers felt that you didn't need to be academically strong to go to music college, whereas you did have to achieve good grades to go to one of the top universities. I did end up going for auditions and interviews at Cambridge, but I decided in the end that music college really was the place for me. Being able to work on my singing one hundred per cent of the time, rather than becoming bogged down in academic work, was the big attraction as I was very clear in my mind, even at this early stage, that it was the singing.

I ended up at the Guildhall School of Music and Drama in a bit of a roundabout way. Initially, I won a place at the Royal Northern College of Music in Manchester and I studied there for a year.

I loved the city socially, but I decided that I was going to have more chances musically if I moved south.

So, I decided to transfer down to London and went straight into the second year at the Guildhall. Jon and Mike were in the second year of their course there and so we became classmates.

The Guildhall felt a little more contemporary and more up to the minute than some of the other colleges where I could have chosen to study. It was exciting to work alongside the drama students there, who were all really cool people. I lived in halls of residence, which was the most educational year of my life and there were plenty of late nights to be had back then. It was great to be with different faces from those I saw every day at college. Nowadays, big nights out are a bit of a rarity because we have to look after ourselves. In this industry, if you go out and get totally drunk, the consequences can impact on your life so much more than in the old days. When you're a student, you can usually get away with it.

The Future

'Looking back, *The X-Factor* was brilliant training for what we're doing now. We're comfortable in TV studios. We know how the whole gig works. We've done an arena tour and a theatre tour. We've made two albums. It's an incredible amount of learning to have crammed into just twelve months.' – MATT

I T'S hard to take in the enormity of what's happened to us in a period of just one year. It has been absolutely incredible. Back in March 2005, we were sitting in our dressing room waiting to go on stage as part of *The X-Factor* Tour. The television was flickering in the corner of the room and we realised that we were about to appear on *Top of the Pops*. We opened a newspaper that happened to be lying on the side and looked at the TV guide. There it was in black and white: '*Top of the Pops*. Including Kaiser Chiefs, J-Lo and G4'.

That took quite a lot of rationalising for the four of us when we saw it for the first time. When you boil it down, we're just four guys from music college who turned up in a practice room for a while, had a bit of

a sing, and then went out for a busk. In the summer of 2004, we were still at college, getting ready to do our final recitals and graduate. It feels like yesterday and so to be where we are now is very, very odd. Even to have one album out, let alone to be releasing two in the space of one year is absolutely incredible. We never ever thought that we would get anywhere near this level. To get on to the live finals of *The X-Factor*, we were so excited. And then to get as high as second place and to meet the chairman of Sony BMG afterwards and to sign for them was amazing. We had no real comprehension of what was going on because everything was happening so quickly.

It's exciting that in years to come, we will be able to show all this stuff to our kids and grandkids and say, 'Your dad did this ...' or 'Your grandad did that...' By then, we will have all gone wrinkly. Right now though, we are determined to enjoy every moment of it.

Our fans range from young kids through to grandparents and all the people in between. It is great to have three generations of one family all listening to the same music.

And lots of the younger people are listening to opera for the first time on our albums.

We have already started to do some promotional work in Europe and we plan to roll that out across the continent over the next few months. Beyond that, we've talked about going even further afield to countries such as Australia and New Zealand. Abroad, people have different tastes in music and we

hope that they will be able to tune into what we do because of the diversity of the songs we sing.

We loved both of the UK tours that we did during 2005 and you can expect to see much more of us out on the road performing live in the very near future. It's what we love doing the most.

We are doing what we are doing because we have always wanted to take our singing and our musicianship to the highest level. We have learned that if you work hard, you get results and that inspires all of us to carry on. In the end, for us, everything has been about the music and, one by one, each of our dreams are coming true. We would never have thought it possible, but we treasure all of these moments along the way. It has all happened so quickly that sometimes we ask ourselves 'Is this the real life? Is this just fantasy?'

The answers are 'Yes' and 'No'. In that order.

Encore

'I love the power a single musical performance has to generate a strong emotional response in people. I find it absolutely incredible and I really love being able to do it at certain times for people. It gives me a tremendous buzz seeing people react in that way.' – JON

'Yes, we did Oasis; we did Britney Spears; we did Radiohead; we did Frank Sinatra; we did Elton John; we did Queen; we did grand opera. That is the most eclectic set of music that has been sung by one group on any talent show ever. And we sung every single one of them live. It wasn't something we set out to do; it was just something that ended up happening. We took risks. After all, it was a massive Saturday night entertainment show and we tried to entertain people.' – MATT

'During the period that *The X-Factor* was on, I lost about a stone and a half because I was expending so much nervous energy. And of the four of us, I think I'm probably the most laid-back. I tend to just take things in my stride. It's been strange because although we were all going through the same thing, we're all very different people with different personalities and we reacted differently to things. It's also been about learning about each other and coping with each other. We're good friends and our relationships have grown by being in G4.' – MIKE

'We occasionally have a few days off here and there, where we can sit and take stock of what's actually gone on. And you ask yourself "What's happened since I last had a holiday?" And you think: I was on this TV show and that TV show; and I sung at this place and that place. And then this new thought goes through your mind: Wow! Did I really do that? And when you're tired and stressed, when you've got an early morning, you just have to realise how lucky you are … how many people would die to be in your situation … and remember what it was that drove you to get there in the first place.' – BEN

Acknowledgements

G4 would like to thank and acknowledge those who have worked with and helped us on our journey so far.

First of all our managers, Louis Walsh and Ashley Tabor at *Walsh Global Management*.

Jo Brock, Jo Davis, Julie Fitzjohn and David Forecast, our fantastic management team.

A special thank you to Gareth Russell, our incredibly dedicated tour manager, who works with us every long hour, every day.

To Tim, Rob, Ged, Nick, Jo, Simon, Andrea and all at *SonyBMG*, you have truly enabled us, we didn't realise how many people it takes behind the scenes at a record company to make dreams happen. Thank you so much. To Ted Cockle, it was a pleasure working with you, thank you for everything and good luck in the future.

To Trevor Horn, Brian Rawling, Graham Stack, Matt Furmidge and all the amazing musicians we have worked with on our album.

To Barbara and Moira at *MBC*, to Solomon and Shaz at *Concorde*, to Barry Clayman, Toby Leighton-Pope, Steve Guest, Florence Stewart and Mike Scoble at *Clear Channel Entertainment*, to Jeremy, Paul and Nick at *Event Merchandising*.

To Faye Sawyer for her amazing work on our styling and for always making us smile!

To Nicole at *Daniel Galvin*.

To Simon Cowell, Sharon Osbourne, Claire Horton, Richard Holloway and everybody who worked with us on *The X Factor*. Thank you so much, we'll never forget those amazing 8 weeks.

To the Guildhall School of Music and Drama

To Stuart, Carolyn and Eleanor at *Virgin Books*, thank you for giving us the opportunity to tell our story in our own words.

To Darren Henley, our co-author, thank you for your dedication, attention to detail and genuine interest in our story and helping us write this book.

And finally, to you the fans for supporting us in every way imaginable. We know it's clichéd, but it's also true, we wouldn't be where we are without you. **Thank You.**